UNCHAINED

RISING ABOVE CHILDHOOD TRAUMA TO FLOURISH IN LIFE, LEADERSHIP, LOVE, AND PARENTING

By

Joshua R. Kennedy

UNCHAINED

RISING ABOVE CHILDHOOD TRAUMA TO FLOURISH IN LIFE, LEADERSHIP, LOVE, AND PARENTING.

JOSHUA R. KENNEDY

CLINICAL THERAPIST/SOCIAL WORKER

Copyright © 2023 by Joshua R. Kennedy. All rights reserved.

This book or any portion of this book may not be reproduced, distributed, or transmitted in any form by any means including photocopying, recording, or other electronic mechanical methods without the express written permission of the publisher. Except in the pace of brief quotations embodied in critical reviews and certain other noncommercial uses permitted by copyright law.

CONTENTS

FOREWARD

My family and I had the privilege of learning about Joshua Kennedy long before our paths crossed. It all began when his father, Aaron, and a dear friend, Abel Wiles, started attending our church. We grew close to them, gaining insight into their trials in Liberia and their arduous journey towards immigration. Our family took on the role of sponsors for the Kennedy family, navigating through numerous twists, challenges, and the stress of the prolonged wait for their arrival. The process unfolded in stages: first Aaron, followed by his wife Mardea, then Joshua and his sister Sieneh, and finally, his older brothers Aaron Jr. and Jimmy. The intricacies and length of this journey, marked by extended family separations, took a toll on the family's well-being. Adding to their struggles were the original traumas that prompted them to leave Liberia in the first place. Upon meeting Joshua and Sieneh at our church, they understandably carried a formal and reserved demeanor in this new cultural setting. However, a defining moment came when Joshua looked up, smiled, and gave me a big eye wink. In that instance, I recognized the strength and spirit within him.

To provide context, our family had previously settled in Worcester, Massachusetts, finding the city to be a mix of positive aspects, such as affordable housing, a low crime rate, and strong schools, juxtaposed with off-putting elements. Historically, Worcester played a leading role in the

5

nation's industrial revolution, attracting European immigrants. However, with the decline of manufacturing, the city faced economic challenges and witnessed minimal migration until crises worldwide brought a wave of immigrants and asylum seekers, including those from Liberia. In the 1990s, Worcester transitioned due to the influx of immigrants, becoming the second-largest destination for immigrants in New England, surpassed only by Boston and offering a more affordable alternative. The city experienced resistance and discrimination towards newcomers, especially those like Joshua, labeled as 'foreigners.' Over time, however, Worcester transformed into a welcoming place, embracing diversity, and appreciating the contributions of immigrants from various corners of the globe.

Joshua's narrative captures the multifaceted nature of the immigrant experience. It goes beyond a mere account of hardships, delving into the emotional tapestry woven by these individuals. The journey encompasses the tangible hurdles faced in their homelands and the intangible aspects, such as the conflicting emotions of relief, joy, wounds, and sorrow associated with leaving behind their familiar roots. It highlights their unwavering faith, courage, and persistence as they seek a new land. It captures the intricate process of beginning afresh, navigating a sea of emotions that include relief, joy, wounds, and sorrow over the departure from their homeland. I hope that as you delve into Joshua's narrative, you will come to appreciate not only his and his family's faith, spirit, and resilience but also gain a deeper insight into the trauma of change, the blessing of adaptation, and the toll these changes take on children who navigate paths that profoundly impact their lives. Through Joshua's narrative, I pray that you find inspiration to embrace change openly and extend a warm welcome to everyone, recognizing that we are all of one accord, endeavoring to survive in this vast and interconnected world.

Dr. Richard Hummel, PhD – Clinical Psychologist

Dr. Richard Hummel, PhD – Clinical Psychologist

DEDICATION

This book offers dedication and a heartfelt tribute to my mother, Mardea Kennedy, and my father, Aaron Kennedy. It's also an embrace extended to the young hearts of Liberia, those who yearn for knowledge today and aspire to shape a brighter and more promising tomorrow for Liberia. To the luminaries of thought, those like Brene Brown, Apostle Joshua Selman, Bishop TD Jakes, the resonant Les Brown, the indomitable Nelson Mandela, and each of you who have chosen to engage with these words, I extend my dedicated gratitude.

In this symphony of inspiration, thankfulness is in order—for the trust and faith you've endowed upon a boy once without hope, who now fervently believes that his voice carries weight. A transformation has occurred amid the embrace of divine providence and human connection. Thus, from the depths of my heart, I thank you all.

INTRODUCTION

Deep within the hidden chambers of our souls, we carry narratives that hold the power to shape and define our very being. Like a masterfully woven tapestry, these stories are as diverse as life. Some threads glisten with the brilliance of joy, love, and triumph. In contrast, others bear the weight of pain, adversity, and heartache. Within this intricate interplay of light and shadow, a profound truth emerges.

Amidst the chapters etched with hues of suffering, tribulation, and turmoil, the most awe-inspiring journey unfurls. Here, the human spirit shines its brightest, for within these very crucibles are the seeds of resilience. Through the depths of despair and the trials that test the limits of our strength, we embark on a transformative expedition—a journey that unveils the depth of our tenacity, the power of healing, and the miracle of metamorphosis. Much like a phoenix rising from the ashes, our spirits learn to mend and rebuild. We discover that healing is not just an act but an art—a masterpiece we paint with every small step toward recovery. The journey itself becomes a canvas, and our hearts wield the brushes of hope and determination.

In such trials, we understand the fragility and strength of human experience. We learn to see beauty in the scars, to find wisdom in the tests, and to recognize the potential for growth within the most daunting challenges. Through these struggles, we uncover our profound resilience—a strength that emerges not despite the pain but because of it. In the symphony of our stories, every note counts—the joyous crescendos and the melancholic refrains alike. Through the sum of our experiences, both luminous and shadowy, we craft the masterpiece of our existence. As we traverse the labyrinthine paths of our lives, we realize that the expedition of tenacity, healing, and metamorphosis is not just a solitary journey—it's a shared testament to the extraordinary strength of the human spirit.

This book delves into the raw and vulnerable terrain of overcoming childhood trauma to unlock a life adorned with boundless possibilities. It navigates the indomitable strength of the human spirit, revealing its unwavering capacity to ascend from even the darkest of shadows. Guided by personal anecdotes, insights, and pragmatic wisdom, this book reveres the potency of vulnerability as it delves into the depths of childhood trauma and its profound repercussions on my journey. Yet, the truth emerges in this exploration—trauma does not serve as our defining essence. Beyond the canvas of our past experiences, we appear as authors, shaping the narratives that grace our existence.

Woven together from a rich tapestry of personal chronicles, professional understanding, and the relentless spirit of humanity, "Unchained" offers a roadmap that unlocks the shackles of childhood trauma. It constructs a path illuminated by empowering strategies and a symphony of heartfelt encouragement, meticulously tailored to those journeying toward healing and personal growth. This literary work embraces the intricate weave of life's complexities, acknowledging that the echoes of childhood traumas reverberate through the corridors of our relationships, leadership expeditions, and the nurturing of generations yet to come. With the author's lived experiences and honed expertise as our guide, we navigate the landscapes of personal growth, resilience, and empowerment. Collectively, we navigate the labyrinth of healing, unveiling the tools and practices that enable us to flourish and thrive, transcending the constraints of our past circumstances.

"Unchained" is a collective call to arms, an invitation extended to a community of kindred souls who grasp the expedition, honor vulnerability, and delight in the triumphant melody of the human spirit. It serves as an anthem, a spirited ode to those who dare to dream, those who forge new narratives, and those who rise to reclaim their intrinsic power. The author's work radiates with the brilliance of his clinical psychology and social services background, a manifestation of his profound desire to uplift the well-being of others. It is grounded in the author's intimate encounters with trauma, loss, mental struggles, and upheaval, acting as the cornerstone of his purpose-driven endeavor. With a distinguished career spanning over fifteen years in human services, the author currently serves the State of Massachusetts, offering unwavering support to children and families navigating the labyrinth of adverse life circumstances. His commitment extends further as a clinical therapist at the Multicultural Wellness Center in Massachusetts, where he provides guidance to families grappling with mental health challenges, traumatic events, pivotal life transitions, academic accomplishments, racial disparities, identity, LGBTQ matters, and the intricacies of academic obstacles.

Drawing wisdom from the experiences of the author's path led him to pen the pages of "Unchained." A resounding truth echoes regardless of the magnitude of one's trauma: its impact permeates every facet of existence. Amidst our trials lies a treasury of lessons waiting to be unearthed. The words of Cheryl Strayed resound, reminding us that our suffering cannot be wished away. It must be confronted, endured, loved, and transcended. Within the crucible of our pain, we discover the bridge to our dreams, erected by our yearning to heal. Within the embrace of this book, the tools to confront our pasts and liberate the inner child seeking validation and recognition within the chaos are unveiled. Sharing our agonies, nightmares, fears, abandonment, and solitude does not render us victims but triumphant victors. The concealed wounds often incite conflicts within, impeding areas of our lives we never foresaw. The author hopes that through his vulnerability and life journey, he can ignite a spark of audacity, fearlessness, authenticity, openness, and courage within others, encouraging them to share their stories and ignite global transformation.

As the author's journey unfurled through the pages of reading, the corridors of learning, the vigilant lens of observation, and the crucible of lived trauma, a luminous realization emerged like a sunrise breaking through the darkness. Traumatic events, like chisels upon the stone of our souls, carve indelible imprints upon the tapestry of our thoughts and feelings. They shape the contours of our lives in profound ways, often eluding our conscious awareness. Crucially, it's paramount to acknowledge that the author doesn't lay claim to wielding universal answers like a master key. This book, rather than dictating a singular right or wrong approach, wisely refrains from prescribing any fixed path for navigating the intricate terrain of trauma, the solitude of loneliness, the delicate dance of mental well-being, the battlefield of warfare, the complexities of parenthood, or the myriad hurdles life presents.

Even the discordant notes of mistakes find their place in the symphony of existence. They hold a sacred, albeit rugged, space in the composition of our lives. These missteps, like alchemists of the soul, transform the base metals of error into the gold of clarity and insight. Thus, even as the graphic horrors of war paint a canvas of pain, suffering, and the echo of loneliness, we emerge from the crucible of adversity with a wisdom that guides us toward a life lived with unapologetic fullness and boundless abundance.

In the wake of engaging with this narrative, the author's aspiration for you is to embody boldness, creativity, innovation, and empowerment. Gaze upon yourself with the same wonder, jubilance, and mandate that you once did. Understand that life's rhythm includes moments of ascension and descent. Yet, we possess the keys to our challenges and solutions in every circumstance. In the unfolding pages of this book, there lies a raw honesty that might stir discomfort in some, for it delves into the depths of human experiences, unfiltered and unapologetic. The brush strokes of my words may paint vivid scenes that some find unsettling, yet there lies a sacred purpose in this tapestry of vulnerability and raw truth.

Just as a ship navigates through stormy waters to reach a distant shore, this book also guides us through the rough seas of our emotions and memories. The turbulence we encounter within these pages is not meant to overwhelm but to empower. Within the very depths of discomfort and disquiet, a transformational journey awaits, leading us to the core of our inner power. Our lives are often shaped by the moments that challenge us, that dare us to confront the shadows within. And it's within these very shadows that our true strength resides, waiting to be acknowledged and harnessed. This book serves as a compass, pointing the way toward our innate resilience and teaching us that even the most painful experiences can be harnessed as catalysts for growth. Just as a diamond is formed under immense pressure, our moments of adversity and trauma can refine us into something more robust and brilliant. This book stands not as a mere collection of words but as a guide that beckons us to journey within, to excavate the strength that lies dormant, waiting to be unearthed.

It's easy to turn away from the uncomfortable and shy away from the stark realities of life. But true transformation is not born in the comfort zone; it emerges from the crucible of challenge. This book invites us to step into that crucible, face our fears and pains head-on, and know that within this confrontation lies the power to transcend. As we navigate the landscapes of our stories, remember that discomfort is not our enemy; it's a signpost along the growth path. As a caterpillar undergoes metamorphosis to become a butterfly, so can we emerge from our trials as remarkable, beautiful, and strong beings. This book is more than just its contents; it's a map that guides us through the labyrinth of our emotions, helping us discover the potential that resides within us, waiting to be realized.

CHAPTER ONE

Chocolate City

The Resilience Of Community Spirit And The Shadow of Loneliness Amidst War

Childhood memories are the foundation upon which our lives are constructed. They're like the pieces of a puzzle that form our identity and connect our youthful selves to the real world. But sometimes, the sad and frightening memories from our past are more significant because they shape how we navigate society as we mature. As Marian Wright Edelman aptly put it, raising children is not the work of a single person; it takes an entire community to do it effectively, regardless of one's financial means. This community support is a sturdy groundwork that our children rely upon. I was fortunate to grow up in a small, tight-knit community known as Chocolate City in Gardnerville, Monrovia, Liberia.

My childhood felt like a thrilling adventure in the heart of Chocolate City. I had many friends, and despite our meals often being limited to just one or two a day, I considered myself exceptionally fortunate. I expressed heartfelt gratitude daily for having both my parents by my side. My father, a revered figure in our community, presided over an elementary school where he tirelessly shaped young minds with his unwavering dedication and wisdom. Meanwhile, my mother's culinary prowess earned her the esteemed title of the finest cook in our neighborhood. To further elevate our family's reputation, my remarkable grandmother left an indelible mark by constructing five public schools and achieving the historic feat of becoming the first female county commissioner in Liberia's Lofa County-ZorZor district. Our family's name was synonymous with respect and admiration within our close-knit world.

In Chocolate City, life thrived on the vibrant interconnectedness of its residents. Our elders were not just mere figures of authority but extensions of our own mothers, and our big brothers and sisters felt like an integral part of our homes. As we roamed the community, the prevailing sense was protection and support, no matter where we ventured. We were a tightly bonded community, united by genuine love and unwavering mutual assistance. Stories and experiences flowed as we gathered. Even in the face of daily trials and the brutal realities of war, our community's spirit of togetherness, love, and unity remained resolute, a powerful force that defied the looming adversities surrounding Chocolate City.

Yet, many challenges lurked beneath the surface of our seemingly joyful existence in Chocolate City. Liberia was gripped by the torment of civil war, a cataclysm that brought a torrent of afflictions. The relentless shadow of illness, heart-wrenching tales of abuse, betrayals that shattered hearts, an enduring sense of sorrow, the never-ending cycle of disappointment, and the persistent ache of loss all hung over our lives like ominous clouds. Amidst this turmoil, our country grappled with surging criminal activities, the haunting specter of death that seemed to shadow our every move, the vice-like grip of poverty that held us in relentless captivity, and the unrelenting suffering etched into the fabric of our daily existence. Pain, abuse, and even the unfathomable torment of torture and rape became harsh realities that our people had to confront daily. During childhood, our perception of the world is profoundly shaped by the values instilled in us by our parents and the nurturing environment in which we are raised. In this regard, I am exceptionally fortunate to have been enveloped in an atmosphere brimming with love, joy, tranquility, and boundless happiness. It was a sanctuary of positivity that stood as a beacon of light amidst the encroaching darkness that engulfed our surroundings.

In life's journey, we often encounter the age-old adage, "Nothing lasts forever." This timeless wisdom reminds us that change is inevitable, and the moments of bliss we savor may be fleeting. During these times of transformation, we realize the true worth of a moment – the realization that its value often becomes most evident when it transforms into a cherished memory. Even in the most trying and dismal of circumstances, there is a treasure we can hold onto: the treasure of our memories. These memories become our guiding stars, illuminating our path through the darkest nights, reminding us of the beauty, love, and joy that once graced our lives, and inspiring us to navigate the present and future challenges with resilience and hope.

The good memories we create as kids stay in our hearts and minds. They're like small guiding lights that shine when facing tough times, like when we go through difficult or painful experiences. When kids go through hard times but quickly bounce back, we call them resilient, which means they're strong and can recover well. Looking back at my time in Chocolate City, I remember some of my happiest memories. These include playing football (soccer), enjoying delicious fruits, and even trying a bit of liquor when I was nine. I had fun playing games and spending time with my dog, Bluebird. I was also fascinated by the stories our "brabiees" (big brothers) shared about the world. These memories were like a source of inner strength for me. They helped me survive and thrive, even when things were challenging. They were like bright spots in my life, reminding me that there was happiness even amid difficulty.

Childhood experiences can be challenging, and many carry hidden pain from our past. Sometimes, we try to forget or ignore these memories, but they can still affect us as adults. Thinking back to my time in Chocolate City, I remember some difficult moments. I saw my best friend drown, and sometimes we played with things we shouldn't have, like human remains. I also witnessed people eating dogs and even other humans. The streets were often filled with dead bodies. I had to go through dangerous situations like alligator-infested waters and bullets flying around. These memories still haunt my dreams. If you talk to most people from my community or other parts of Liberia, you'll hear stories that would shock you. Living there was far from easy. It was hard to tell who was good and evil because everyone was trying to survive. But the important thing is that we, the survivors, have a message of hope. Despite all the darkness we faced, we can still share our stories and support one another. It reminds us to cherish the moments of peace and safety we have now and to work together to create a world where no one has to endure such hardships. We can find strength in our shared experiences and help each other heal.

As children, when we witness the harsh realities of life, we go through a process that many don't fully understand. Some children act out in school, some withdraw and isolate themselves, and others grapple with various mental health challenges that can even lead to thoughts of suicide. However, many, if not most, children try to push that trauma aside and move forward as if it didn't affect them, the resilient ones. They may not realize that these traumas can manifest in various aspects of their lives. These impacts can show up in their decision-making abilities, causing indecisiveness. It can affect their relationships with family, friends, and loved ones. Even their roles as leaders or parents can be influenced by their past traumas, often because they deny or are unaware of how these experiences have shaped them. But here's the critical part: recognizing these effects is the first step toward healing and personal growth. By acknowledging the past and its impact on our present, we can work to make positive changes in our lives. It's a journey toward better decision-making, healthier relationships, and becoming more effective leaders and parents. Remember, understanding your past can be the key to a brighter future.

As children, we hear about neighbors and loved ones losing their lives daily. Sons would harm their mothers and sisters, and fathers would do unthinkable things to their families, all in a desperate bid for survival. It was a time of unimaginable hardship. Friends I grew up with went missing for weeks, if not months, and returned holding a gun. Young children who had the strength to carry guns, machetes, knives, or any other tools had a better chance of surviving to see the next day compared to those who refused to take up arms. It was a stark reality of those challenging times. Every breath I took felt like a blessing because fear was everywhere in my country. During those dark times, we had to hide. In our hiding, we would hear heartbreaking stories of mothers and daughters enduring daily horrors. Their bodies were treated as playthings by men who carried weapons and wielded strength to take advantage of them. It was a terrifying reality. Families who ventured out to find food for their loved ones didn't return whole. Some came back missing limbs, ears, or other body parts; sadly, some never returned. We would hear disturbing stories about soldiers and men using women's private parts in rituals, believing they would grant them tremendous strength, power, and even invincibility against bullets. We heard pregnant women were in high demand because their unborn babies, sometimes cut open from their bellies and given for ritual purposes to witch doctors, made everyday men leaders of their rebel forces due to the power they possessed from ripping an unborn child from a mother's womb. We would hear unsettling stories of soldiers wearing women's private parts around their necks and engaging in cannibalistic acts. These tales haunted us as we hid from the horrors, finding solace in the love of those around us but still feeling profoundly lonely within ourselves.

In every corner of our existence, death cast its ominous shadow. The nights were punctuated by the loud crack of gunfire, and as we lay in our beds, fear was our constant companion. The dawn often brought the heart-rending sounds of mothers and fathers grieving for their lost loved ones. The community stood as a beacon of hope amidst the darkness of those times. However, while the community's solidarity shielded us from some of the horrors of war, hunger emerged as an insidious adversary. It nibbled at our very existence, threatening to snuff out the flickering flame of life. Surviving meant eating whatever scraps we could find - grass, drinking dirty water, or whatever fragments we could salvage from trash cans. Hunger became a silent executioner, claiming lives with ruthless efficiency.

Amid this desperate struggle, my father, once a robust figure at two hundred and forty pounds, withered away to a mere ninety-five pounds. Our daily sustenance often amounted to no more than a spoonful of rice or a sip of swamp water. It felt like life had drained away, leaving a desolate landscape of despair. As we lay down to sleep each night, the encroaching fear whispered that our end was near. Yet, within this seemingly relentless darkness, a spark of resilience flickered. The enduring spirit of our community, its unwavering love and unity, provided a glimmer of hope. Despite the dire circumstances, we held on to the belief that better days would come. It was a testament to the strength of the human spirit, a reminder that even in the face of unimaginable adversity, we can find the courage to endure and the will to keep moving forward.

However, as children in Chocolate City, these experiences felt strangely normal because they were all we knew. We were surrounded by these harsh realities every day, and our primary concerns were often simple yet vital: finding food, accessing clean water, and hoping that we'd live to see another day. As I matured, I came to understand the profound trauma experienced by myself and millions of children in Liberia, recognizing how deeply it has shaped our lives. As this understanding settled in, I asked myself, "Why is our world so filled with darkness and suffering?" It's a question that may cross your mind too, especially when life delivers its harshest blows to you or someone you care about. Life in Chocolate City had its ups and downs, a bittersweet blend. I hold dear the days spent with my friends—playing marbles and football, relishing in the sweetness of ripe mangoes, swaying under the plum tree's branches, and losing ourselves in games of hide and seek. These memories, like precious treasures, have etched themselves deeply into my life, leaving an indelible mark. Yet amidst the joy, there lingered darker moments—ones we sought to bury or turn a blind eye to. These experiences, though we may strive to forget them, have nonetheless shaped our paths in ways we grapple to comprehend. Once, I thought the brightness of our shared laughter could overpower the shadows of those painful recollections. Yet, there remain memories we actively choose to shroud, for they carry with them the weight of sorrow, loneliness, and the ache of remembrance. While loneliness is often something we strive to evade, the memories we ignore can stealthily infiltrate our relationships, our interactions in social settings, our capacity to forge connections, our courage to express ourselves, and even our sense of identity. Yet, amidst this sobering reality lies an empowering truth: confronting these neglected memories and their impact on us marks the inaugural stride toward healing and personal evolution. By bravely confronting our past and its enduring sway over our present, we embark on a journey toward cultivating more meaningful connections, amplifying our voices, and aligning with our authentic selves. Remember, even in life's most daunting junctures, there exists a beacon of hope guiding us toward a brighter tomorrow.

Loneliness, often hidden away like a closely guarded secret, profoundly influences our lives. It can shape how we love, make decisions, and ultimately how we live our lives. Yet, it remains a topic that we as a society tend to tiptoe around. We conceal it, believing that our loneliness is our burden, a secret others ignore. In reality, loneliness is a universal emotion, a thread that weaves its way through the tapestry of human experience. As a renowned psychologist and author, Jordan Peterson, aptly says, "You don't get to choose not to be hurt in this world, but you do have some say in who hurts you." For me, the first encounter with loneliness came at the tender age of eleven. It was a perplexing sensation, difficult to grasp and even harder to articulate. It felt like being adrift in a vast world, utterly isolated despite being surrounded by people—hundreds, even thousands of them. A sense of not belonging consumed me. My words seemed to evaporate into thin air, stifled by an unseen force. Speaking became a futile endeavor, as if everyone was against me, driving me further into silence.

In contemplating the complex interplay between loneliness and our lives, the insights of Brené Brown, a research professor and author, offer invaluable perspective. She notes, "Imperfections are not inadequacies; they are reminders that we're all in this together." Loneliness, often rooted in inadequacy or unworthiness, underscores the inherent human condition of imperfection. It is a shared experience that transcends individual boundaries. The belief that we must bear the weight of our loneliness alone is a fallacy. We are not alone in feeling this way; countless others have navigated these turbulent waters. When left unaddressed, loneliness can become a formidable force influencing every facet of our existence. It casts a shadow over our capacity to love, forge meaningful connections, and make decisions that align with our true selves. Dr. Gabor Maté, a renowned physician and expert in addiction, eloquently emphasizes the link between our emotional well-being and our actions: "Stress doesn't only make us feel awful emotionally. It can also exacerbate just about any health condition you can think of." As a potent form of emotional stress, loneliness profoundly impacts our mental and physical well-being. It can trigger heightened anxiety, deepen feelings of depression, and foster a pervasive sense of disconnection, ultimately shaping our decisions and actions in ways we may not anticipate.

As I've come to understand, our struggle with loneliness transcends age, race, or circumstance. The perception that our loneliness is an isolated experience, unique to ourselves, is an illusion that hinders us from seeking the support and understanding we truly need. In the words of Oprah Winfrey, a renowned media mogul and philanthropist, 'The more you praise and celebrate your life, the more there is in life to celebrate.' We must not only celebrate moments of joy and connection but also acknowledge and embrace moments of vulnerability and loneliness, for they are an integral part of the human experience. By acknowledging our loneliness and reaching out for support, we create the space for healing and growth to thrive.

CHAPTER 2

Daybreak

Unmasking Trauma, Embracing Vulnerability, And

Healing The Soul

T he repercussions of unresolved trauma wield a formidable power, exacting a toll far beyond what meets the eye. Its insidious fingers grip our habits, twisting our perspective on life into contorted shapes. The consequences ripple through our existence, imprinting themselves upon our very DNA. Peter A. Levine aptly states, 'The effects of unresolved trauma can have devastating consequences." Such repercussions sow the seeds of addiction, cloud our decision-making like a fog of confusion, and cast a shadow over the sanctity of family life and the tapestry of relationships we weave.

But it doesn't stop there. Like a silent storm, unresolved trauma doesn't shy away from the physical realm. It unfurls its dark banner, brandishing real physical pain, tangible symptoms, and even the specter of disease. Its grip tightens, manifesting its presence not only in the depths of our psyche but within the very fibers of our being. Yet, amid this storm, there is a glimmer of revelation, a pathway to freedom. We find ourselves grappling with these unhealthy thoughts and emotions, the echoes of early traumas that have woven themselves into the fabric of our existence. As we trace back the root cause of the chaos that holds our lives captive, a vital truth emerges – the significance of understanding the turmoil within is often hard to face.

In facing our trauma head-on, we encounter internal skirmishes rivaling titans' battles. The storm within can seem too tumultuous to face directly. We sometimes attempt to quell the storm with external diversions. A party here, an illicit substance there, or even engaging in destructive confrontations, like a leaf caught in a vortex. In my journey, I grappled with a particular storm: womanizing, seeking solace in the fleeting connections that left me more adrift than anchored. The journey to healing and wholeness begins with acknowledging that true change isn't merely altering external behaviors. It requires an inner transformation, a reckoning with the storm that rages within. Like an alchemist, we must transmute the pain into growth, the suffering into strength, and the chaos into clarity. The very storms that once threatened to tear us asunder can be harnessed to propel us toward a life lived in the fullness of purpose, and the boundless freedom of the soul.

In the crucible of addressing our trauma from within, we forge a connection with our true selves, stripped of the shackles that trauma had cast upon us. Trauma, a cunning adversary, casts its shadow across various facets of our existence, coercing us into decisions that deviate from our inherent nature. It's as if we're caught in a storm, grappling with emotions and choices that stand at odds with the person we know ourselves to be.

When trauma strikes in our formative years, its impact weaves a complex tapestry of suppression. We bury the weighty emotions and experiences, shoving them into the recesses of our consciousness. Yet, this concealment begets an insidious transformation, breeding negativity, self-censure, and emotional afflictions. The scars of trauma morph into barriers that birth depression, alienate us from society, and birth an ever-pervasive sense of anxiety. This internal conflict births an antagonist within – the 'inner voice.' It echoes with self-destructive narratives, a chorus of doubt sabotaging our essence.

The journey within to confront and heal is not linear but marked by formidable battles. The inner critic, armed with the weaponry of past pain, perpetuates the cycle of isolation and uncertainty. Feelings of sorrow and estrangement are its weapons, urging us to relinquish human connection, surrender to sadness, and exist in perpetual doubt. When the storm of the COVID-19 pandemic swept across the globe, I, like many, was confronted with the specters of my past that I had so deftly hidden away. The solitude imposed by confinement became an unforgiving mirror, reflecting the prison of suppressed emotions. The pandemic laid bare the fears I had long disregarded, forcing me to confront them head-on. The veneer I had meticulously crafted began to crumble within my two-bedroom apartment, shared with my girlfriend and two sons. The days were painted with the joy of playing with my sons, yet the nights bore witness to the resurgence of nightmares rooted in childhood trauma. Routines, once steadfast, unraveled in the face of uncertainty. Loneliness, which is like the darkness of connection, became my friend. My journey of survival and the perils that entail survivorship made me feel like an outsider in any room I ventured. However, during the pandemic, I felt caged in the presence of love.

In those moments, my friend, let me paint a vivid picture for you. The edges of my sanity began to blur, fading into the nebulous abyss of my mind. The familiar tools of distraction and evasion, which I had clung to so desperately, suddenly lost their once-potent charm. They crumbled like sandcastles before an incoming tide, leaving me standing on the shifting sands of my own uncertainty. I felt lost and profoundly out of place like an actor stumbling upon an unfamiliar stage with no script, cues, or audience to guide me.

The escape I had often found solace in, the comforting presence of women, was no longer possible because fear had draped its oppressive shroud over everyone, immobilizing even the most routine of movements. I was trapped in a cocoon of isolation, a prisoner of solitude. It was as if the world had collectively held its breath, and I, too, had been swept into this suffocating stillness. Internally, a storm raged. My emotions churned like a whirlpool; their turbulence heightened by the enforced confinement of my surroundings. I felt explosively quiet within, a profound silence that drowned out the thoughts and worries that usually swirled in my mind. It was like trying to hold back a tidal wave with a mere bucket – futile indeed. The emotional deluge threatened to overwhelm me, and I was ill-equipped to contain it.

There I stood, exposed and vulnerable, with no place to hide, no refuge from the torrents of emotions that crashed relentlessly upon the shores of my soul. It was as if the universe had chosen this moment to place a magnifying glass over my pain, illuminating it in ways I could no longer ignore. My feelings' raw, unfiltered intensity laid bare the depths of my vulnerability, forcing me to confront the essence of who I was and what I had become. In those trying times, my friend, I was pushed to the brink of my understanding, caught between the chaos of the world and the tumultuous seas of my psyche.

Oh, the darkness of night, my friend, became both my confidant and tormentor. In the stillness, in the silent hours when the world was wrapped in slumber, I was left alone with my thoughts, memories, and self. And there, within the confines of my own mind, a reckoning awaited – a moment of decision that held the weight of eternity. My path ahead, my friend, seemed like a treacherous journey through a dense forest of uncertainty. The wind whispered doubts, the shadows cast their own shadows, and the thorns of fear seemed ready to ensnare my every step. It was a path that demanded courage of the highest order, resilience that could bend but not break. Depressive thoughts and relentless darkness descend upon my thoughts – a darkness that whispers poisonous notions of unworthiness, brokenness, loneliness, and lovelessness. These insidious thoughts, like vengeful specters, haunted my every waking moment. As I closed my eyes, sleep slipped further away, replaced by a nightmare realm where human remains were grotesquely stitched together, their anguished voices forming a haunting chorus that called out my name. In those haunting visions, I saw eyes being gouged, limbs being severed, and unspeakable violence upon humans were done. It was like a pot of soup of blood with so much meat of human remains boiling with laughter and adulation. I couldn't fathom the moment of darkness as a discord of voices pierced the silence I sought, each bearing names I could not recall and whispering a reminder of the unrelenting trauma I bore witness to.

As my inner struggles intensified, my external world began to crumble around me. The cozy confines of my apartment, once filled with cherished memories of my girlfriend and sons, transformed into a battleground. Our arguments mirrored the chaos within me, with my focus shifting to my partner's perceived flaws while ignoring my own imperfections. This internal conflict took a tangible toll on our relationship, leading to a growing disconnect between us. The once harmonious atmosphere of our home now echoed with tension, culminating in my partner's plea for space and separation. Behind a forced smile or a hollow laugh, I concealed the shattered pieces of my heart, broken by confusion and profound loneliness.

Oh, my friend, I can feel the weight of that moment in the very fibers of my soul. It's as if time stood still, and all that remained was the echo of her voice, the urgency in her plea. There's a sacredness in those moments when the universe beckons us to awaken, when the cries of those we love to become a clarion call that we can no longer ignore. I remember it vividly – her eyes, like windows to her soul, reflecting a torment I had become blind to. It was as if every tear she had ever shed and every silent prayer she had whispered into the night was laid bare at that moment. Her words, sharp as a dagger, "Get out of my life. I can't do this anymore!" They pierced through the façade I had so carefully constructed, the mask that concealed my pain and the wreckage I had unintentionally left in my wake.

At that moment, her words echoed like a haunting refrain. I had heard those words from her lips before, but they had an unmistakable gravity this time. She wasn't speaking in jest or offering vague hints; her words were laced with sincerity, and her stance exuded a resolute determination. Once warm and playful, her tone had transformed into a direct and unwavering declaration. She left no room for ambiguity or misinterpretation. It was as if she had gathered all her unspoken thoughts and emotions and distilled them into this decisive moment. And then, there were her eyes—those windows to her soul. They bore into me with a sharpness rivaling an eagle's keen gaze, piercing through any defenses I might have had left. In her eyes, I saw the intensity of her emotions, the weight of her decision, and the resolve behind her words. With her broad shoulders squared, she walked away, each step marked by a confidence and prowess I had always admired. Her departure was deliberate, a testament to her newfound clarity and determination. Her reminder cut through the air like a blade as she turned again to face me. She emphasized that what we had shared until that point was not genuine, that it had been a mirage built on uncertainty and half-hearted commitment.

The word "situationship" hung in the air, encapsulating the ambiguity and emotional limbo that had defined our connection. At that moment, I felt a mixture of regret, surprise, and a dawning realization that I had taken the woman I had come to love for many years for granted. Her honesty and courage to end what wasn't working, despite any discomfort or pain it might bring, left me with a profound sense of respect for her. It was a turning point, a moment of clarity when the line between what we had been and what we could be had been decisively drawn.

It's a haunting realization, my friends, when you understand that your own turmoil and battles can become the storm that engulfs those you hold closest. In my pursuit of masking my inner storms, I had inadvertently created a hurricane that swept away the foundation of love and companionship I cherished. But let me tell you, my friend, a moment of grace emerges from the ashes of such revelations. It's a moment when you stand face to face with the truth and see yourself not through your own struggles but through the eyes of those who love you. However, the mask I wore wasn't just a shield I held up for the world; it was a barricade that kept the woman who cherished me at arm's length.

My internal battle had been a blinding storm, obscuring the truth from my sight like thick, impenetrable clouds. I was caught amid a flurry of conflicting thoughts and emotions, unable to find a clear path forward. It was as if I had been stumbling through the darkness, unable to discern the right course. But, as they say, "the chicken crows in the morning," and so it was that the dawn of realization broke upon me. Just as the birds began to chirp and sing, their joyful melodies resonating in the early light, I felt a newfound clarity seep into my consciousness. The screeching of my internal struggles faded, like the owls retreating from the encroaching day. With the rising sun, a sense of awakening washed over me. It was a new day, a fresh start, and I could see the truth I had been avoiding. The internal battle had served its purpose, leading me to this moment of enlightenment. I woke up to the reality of the situation and the potential for growth and transformation ahead.

It was the undeniable truth that had always been there, waiting for me to see it – the truth that facing the echoes of my past was not just a choice, but a necessity. A necessity to liberate my present from the chains of yesterday, a need to carve a future that was no longer dictated by the shadows that once held me captive. And in that acknowledgment, my friend, something powerful was set in motion – the seeds of transformation were sown. You see, acknowledging the pain, trauma, and scars was like planting seeds in the fertile soil of my heart. These were not seeds of despair but seeds of resilience. With each acknowledgment, each step towards the core of my past, the roots of these seeds began to dig deep. They dug deep into the layers of my pain, into the soil of my history, and in that very digging, they unearthed the raw materials for my healing.

As my relationship crumbled and the new day dawned, I was entangled in a fierce internal battle that challenged deeply ingrained cultural perceptions about masculinity and vulnerability. For years, I had been conditioned to believe that I should not show weakness, shed tears, or display any form of vulnerability as a man. Society had reinforced that men must weather internal and external struggles with relentless vigor and unyielding strength. But, my friends, at that moment, I stood at a crossroads where the threads of my cultural upbringing, personal identity, and the harsh reality of my situation converged. The loneliness and the overwhelming thoughts that clouded my mind became unbearable, pushing me to seek solace and guidance from a higher power. As a devout Pentecostal Christian, I dressed in my all-white attire, symbolizing purity and surrender, and cried out to God. I poured out my heart in my prayers and fasting, seeking clarity and direction amidst the chaos that engulfed my life.

During this spiritual journey, a powerful realization began to stir within me—recognizing that the profound darkness I encountered could no longer be concealed or dealt with in isolation. It demanded nothing less than the illuminating power of truth. With a reservoir of courage, I didn't know I possessed, I made a pivotal decision. I chose to cast aside the cloak of secrecy that had shrouded my struggles and fears. Despite my initial reluctance to reveal the depths of my inner turmoil to the public eye, I took a bold step forward. In a moment of vulnerability, I reached out to my pastor, a beacon of wisdom and empathy within my faith community.

As our conversation unfolded, time seemed to stretch, enveloping us in a sacred cocoon where the unrest of my soul found its voice. For what felt like hours, though it could have been an eternity, he stood as an unwavering pillar of strength, a beacon of solace amid the storm of my emotions. In his presence, I unraveled the intricate tapestry of turmoil that had woven itself into the very essence of my being. His attentive listening and unwavering support, devoid of judgment, illuminated the profound power of human connection in moments of vulnerability. Opening myself to him was an act of surrender—a relinquishing of pride, fears, and the isolation I had imposed upon myself. It was in this surrender that I discovered a newfound strength, a strength that came not from guarding my vulnerabilities but from embracing them. The wisdom of my pastor's words and the warmth of his understanding created a haven where my pain was no longer confined to the shadows. Still, they allowed me to enter the light.

In that sacred exchange, I learned that healing begins when we shed the armor of silence and allow ourselves to be seen in our entirety. My pastor's presence was a living testament to the truth that sharing our burdens with a compassionate soul can be a transformative act that leads to relief and ultimately, to the path of healing. In his attentive listening, I found solace and validation—a validation of the importance of seeking help, embracing vulnerability, and embarking on a journey of self-discovery that would forever alter the course of my life. I emerged from that conversation not only lighter, having released the weight of my pain, but also empowered by the realization that seeking help is not a sign of weakness but a testimony to our resilience.

After our initial exchange, my pastor proposed a weekly rendezvous to discuss whatever I wished to share. I embraced the opportunity, sensing it as a chance to embark on a transformative journey paved by the wisdom of scripture. Week after week, I sat with my pastor as he imparted relevant biblical verses and recounted tales of significant figures like Joseph, Moses, Job, David, Esther, and the ultimate embodiment of love and redemption, Jesus Christ. These sessions became an oasis of solace, akin to sipping comforting tea on a wintry day—soothing, rejuvenating. Gradually, I discerned that this liaison with my pastor, who was skilled in counseling trauma victims through the prism of biblical teachings, was a wise decision. His guidance, woven with the tapestry of scriptural wisdom, offered a fresh lens through which to view my struggles. The triumphs, the endurance, and the redemption encapsulated in the tales of old bible stories became a wellspring of hope and inspiration. These timeless stories reinforced that my pain wasn't unique, and that transformation and healing were attainable.

With my pastor's unwavering presence as my anchor, I embarked on the labyrinthine passages of my trauma. Guided by biblical principles, my pastor and I navigated the terrain of forgiveness, resilience, and the incandescent power of faith to surmount adversity. The sessions transformed into sacred spaces where I could confront my past, process my emotions, and unchain myself from the abyss that gripped me. As weeks melted into months, I witnessed the metamorphic potency of faith intertwined with counseling. The murky clouds that had shrouded my existence dissipated, replaced by the faint glow of hope and a rekindled sense of purpose. My relationship with the Divine deepened. I discerned the profound embrace of love and grace, essential ingredients in my pilgrimage toward healing.

Please make no mistake, my friends; the path of confronting one's past is not one paved with rose petals. It's a journey that demands vulnerability, the laying bare of wounds we'd rather keep hidden. It's a journey that challenges our notions of who we are and who we can be. Yet, within this challenge lies the opportunity for metamorphosis. Just as a caterpillar must surrender to the cocoon to emerge as a butterfly, we must submit to confronting our demons to rise as champions of our own narrative. So, if we find ourselves at that crossroads, my friend, know this: we are not alone. The journey may seem overwhelming, and the darkness may appear impenetrable, but within us lies a wellspring of strength we never knew existed. With each step we take towards facing our past, we are an inch closer to reclaiming our present and shaping a future that is no longer imprisoned by the chains of yesterday. It won't be easy; no transformation ever is, but the rewards are boundless – the freedom to live authentically, the power to rewrite our story, and the joy of discovering the warrior within us.

However, let's acknowledge the intricate and unpredictable nature of the transformative process. Like a meandering river, it twists and turns, sometimes flowing steadily and at other times churning with turbulence. Understanding this nonlinear journey allows us to navigate its twists and turns with greater resilience and grace. Along the winding path of self-discovery, setbacks may cast shadows, old wounds may stir from their slumber, and unforeseen challenges may emerge. Yet, amidst the unpredictable currents of this journey, the tools we gather become a stalwart shield against the relentless tide of adversity. I've come to realize that self-care isn't mere indulgence—it's a sacred commitment to honoring the vessel that houses our spirit. By carving out moments of stillness, extending the kindness of self-compassion, and seeking guidance from professionals when needed, we weave threads of resilience into the intricate tapestry of our ongoing voyage toward growth and holistic well-being. Moreover, my voyage of healing has unveiled a profound truth: my personal odyssey is intricately interwoven with the universal healing of our human family. As we grapple with the far-reaching ramifications of trauma, we become the architects of a world drenched in empathy and understanding. With each step toward self-awareness, I dismantle the internal adversary that seeks to trap me. It's a journey of unity, where our collective spirit ignites a luminary flame that pierces through the darkness within, dispelling it with the radiant force of agreement and audacious courage.

In this juncture of reflection, I am grateful for the courage to seek help and the faith that sustained me through the ordeal. The fusion of therapy grounded in scripture, unwavering encouragement from my pastor, and the teachings of Jesus unfurled my path to healing. Freed from the shackles of my past and the constraints of societal norms, I now stand as a testament to the power of confronting cultural restraints and breaking free from imposed limitations. Reclaiming my birthright—to heal, flourish, and live authentically—has been a journey of liberation. And I'm not alone in this journey; my story serves as a ripple, inspiring others to break free from societal molds and embrace identities founded on conviction rather than conformity. Seeking help isn't a sign of weakness; it's a testament to one's resilience and the love they hold for themselves.

CHAPTER 3

Thief Of The Night

Confronting The Shadows Of Sexual Abuse And Reclaiming Our Light

I carry with me a story that has long dwelled in the shadows of my soul. Throughout the expanse of my existence, a profound apprehension has held me captive, shackling my spirit and chaining my voice. For countless years, I've borne the fear of merciless judgment, scornful laughter, heartless stereotypes, damning labels, and the dread of becoming a topic of discussion in hushed tones.

I stand before you today as a man who has walked hand in hand with hundreds of fellow human beings, both men and women, who have been victims of the unspeakable horror that is sexual abuse. In my humble opinion, our society has struggled, and continues to struggle, to offer a compassionate and constructive response to the scourge of sexual abuse, particularly when it inflicts its profound wounds upon the souls of men. My journey has led me through a labyrinth of research, a quest marked by the study of case histories, the heartfelt narratives of survivors shared through testimonial videos, the profound wisdom inscribed within books, and soul-baring conversations with those who have survived the indescribable. Through this odyssey, I have come to a disheartening realization— an unsettling lack of clarity shrouds the intricate web of why sexual abuse occurs, why each and every one of us stands vulnerable to its sinister grasp, how to address it when it casts its ominous shadow, and most importantly, the path to healing and redemption that awaits those who have been ensnared by its malevolent force.

Regardless of the manifold facets of our identity—be it race, gender, age, or sexual orientation, none among us is immune to the lurking specter of sexual abuse. It haunts the corridors of our lives, ever watchful, ever ready to pounce upon the unsuspecting. This is the harsh truth we must confront, for only in acknowledging our shared vulnerability can we hope to stand united against this pervasive menace. My unwavering belief, deeply rooted in the soil of my experiences and nurtured by the wisdom of countless survivors, is that trauma stands as the sinister force propelling the grotesque machinery of sexual abuse, molestation, mental and emotional torment, and the numbing escape into the abyss of substance abuse. It is a haunting irony that those who inflict these deep wounds upon others often bear their own unhealed scars of trauma, a cruel legacy that compels them to perpetrate the cycle of suffering.

In the sentences that follow, I embarked upon a deeply personal journey of empowerment and the reclamation of my inner light. Today marks the first time I summon the courage to acknowledge and inscribe this facet of my life. For far too long, I've veiled this traumatic chapter, shrouding it in secrecy, driven by the gnawing tendrils of shame and guilt that coiled around my heart. I bore this burden silently, convinced that somehow, it was my own fault, my own doing. The wounds of that bruised, frightened child within me festered, unhealed, and unseen. The trauma I endured was a weighty burden I chose to carry alone, hidden from the world's gaze because I believed myself to be tainted, sullied by an event that was never my fault. The tendrils of guilt coiled around my heart, squeezing it ever so tightly, as if blaming myself could somehow turn back the hands of time.

When a wound festers untreated, it doesn't simply stay the same; it deepens and spreads, both within us and in the way our lives unfold. The pain that simmers beneath the surface eventually finds its way into the open, often in ways we're blind to or choose to deny. For over two decades, my wounds remained exposed, an open abyss that kept me separated from my own self. They rendered me invisible to my own being. Over the course of the past three decades, I engaged in a relentless pursuit of escape, running from the turmoil within. I shuffled from place to place, job to job, and relationship to relationship, hoping that the change in external circumstances would somehow mend what was broken within me. These choices, well-intentioned but misguided, led to the blessing of three remarkable sons, each from a different mother. Yet, in my quest for healing, I often acted recklessly, seeking solace in parties, forming ill-fated connections with sexual partners, and making decisions that only served to compound my pain. Bessel A. van der Kolk once wisely stated, "As long as you keep secrets and suppress information, you are fundamentally at war with yourself…The critical issue is allowing yourself to know what you know. That takes an enormous amount of courage."

There are moments in life, certain events, that etch themselves into the very fabric of our conscious minds, and they hold the power to unravel our existence. In November 1999, on a somber, overcast weekday, I found myself in a situation where I had no one to play with. You see, at that time, I was homeless, and my nights were spent seeking refuge in abandoned houses. On that particular day, I sought shelter in my neighbor's taxi, which was conveniently parked on the field where we often played football (or soccer). Draped in my mother's clothes, I huddled inside the car, my thoughts consumed by the absence of my mother who had embarked on a journey to the United States.

As I lay there, tears welled up in my eyes, and I began to cry. I cried not just tears but deep, heart-wrenching sobs that seemed to emanate from the very core of my being. I cried until exhaustion overcame me, and I drifted into an uneasy slumber. When I awoke, the world was eerily silent; there was no familiar sound of roosters heralding the dawn. The night was gradually giving way to the approaching daylight. You see, I had spent countless nights in my neighbor's car, but this time was different. This time, fear gripped me as I opened my eyes to the half-light.

I clutched at myself, pulling my meager coverings tighter around my shivering form, praying for the first rays of daylight to come to my rescue. The car, a mere shell of its former self, lacked a windshield, tires, or an engine. It left me exposed, vulnerable, and utterly terrified. I was consumed by a fear that had haunted my childhood - the fear of witchcraft. In our community, there was talk of an older lady, a mysterious figure who many believed had the power to fly on a broom in the dead of night. As I lay there, trembling in the darkness, I couldn't help but imagine that this sinister witch might come for me. I clenched my fists, my toes, and my eyes shut tight as if that could shield me from the encroaching darkness. I could see nothing but blackness, and the eerie calls of owls and the rustling of nocturnal animals served as an unsettling lullaby.

A few minutes passed, and amidst the eerie silence, a melodic voice filled the air, singing a gospel song. The sound pierced through the darkness, and I impulsively opened my eyes, straining to identify the person behind the voice. Carefully, I peeked outside, and my gaze settled on a figure that resembled my neighbor, yet uncertainty clouded my judgment. I raised my head slightly, squinting in the dim light, and he seemed to sense my scrutiny. He called out, "Who's there?" My lips remained sealed; I dared not utter a word, caught between the familiarity of the voice and the persistent fear of the witch lady's deception. As I hesitated, the car door creaked open, and a massive hand reached in, grabbing at my shirt. Panic surged through me, and I began to shout, "Help! Help! Help!" But before I could scream further, he silenced me with a chilling threat, "I have a gun. If you open your mouth again, I will shoot you." I was paralyzed with fear, confined to the car, my head bowed between my legs, thoughts racing, and a terrifying realization settling in - I believed I was about to die.

The ability to scream had deserted me; I didn't even know how to. My heart pounded in my chest, and my legs felt as if they were anchored to the ground. He took hold of my jaw, demanding to know the whereabouts of my older brothers. All I could do was cry quietly, the tears mingling with my silent prayers. He probed further, asking why my brothers had allowed me to sleep in this decrepit car when my father was in America, and we had a school of our own. My tearful response was laden with fear, "The woman who was taking care of us kicked me out and said we couldn't go back to my father's school or our own house." His interrogation continued, "Where are your brothers?" In my terrified state, I had no answers to offer, and I stammered, "I don't know." He commanded me to return to the car, his tone was authoritative, his silhouette casting an ominous figure with a hidden gun and his imposing, camouflaged frame. He resembled my neighbor, he sounded like him, but the specter of the witch still loomed larger in my mind, casting doubt over this encounter.

I slowly eased myself into the car, preparing to close the door when I noticed him turning around. He was clad in a red camouflage shirt, gray khaki pants, and black flip-flops. He stood by the car door, and as my gaze met his, I saw his eyes, red as burning embers, and detected the unmistakable scent of marijuana emanating from him. Panic surged within me, and I attempted to exit the car, but his large hands clamped around my throat, pushing me forcefully to the ground. At that moment, I thought to myself, "I am going to die." In that horrifying instant, I found myself robbed of the ability to cry out, yell, or even speak. I felt a strange numbness as he forced his penis into my mouth, all the while holding his gun menacingly to my head. He thrust violently, and I struggled to comprehend what was happening. Desperately, I began to think of my mother, and her name became a mantra, repeating itself in my mind, "Mama, mama,

mama, mama." Yet, my feeble resistance persisted. I tried to close my mouth, biting down on his penis in a desperate attempt to fight back. In response, he recoiled sharply, striking me across the face with the pistol. I fell to my left side, and he issued a chilling warning, "If you bite me, you'll never see your mother and father again." Still, I continued to battle, my understanding of the situation fogged by confusion and fear.

He seized me and flung me forward into the car, where I lay prone on my face, my legs subjected to his brutal kicks. My pleas filled the air, "What are you doing? What are you doing? I will tell my brothers." But he showed no mercy. He pounced on top of me, his left hand covering my mouth, and thrusting his penis into me with no avail. He continues thrusting his penis over and over, but I kept on fighting, I do not know where the courage or strength came from, but I kept moving my hips and kicking my legs. I felt his penis arching up my anal but my movement and kicking made him angrier and he punch me in the buttock and grab my throat. The terror that gripped me was overwhelming; I believed I was facing imminent death. I fought back with every ounce of strength I could muster, but he was overpowering. Tears streamed down my face as I cried uncontrollably. Finally, he withdrew, and I heard the roosters crowing in the distance. Still, he wasn't finished. He seized my head, pressed the pistol against my jaw, and issued a final chilling threat, "If you say anything about this, I will come and kill you, and you'll never see your mother and father again." With a final act of brutality, he slapped my legs and fled into the darkness.

I lay there, unable to feel anything. My entire body was numb, and I sobbed uncontrollably. It was then that the daughter of the neighbor, in whose car I had sought refuge, found me. She extended an invitation to eat eggs at their home, and I accepted, all the while harboring a deep fear and uncertainty about my future. On that very day, I managed to speak to my mother, though I cannot recall how I sounded or what words I used. I implored her to allow me to come to the United States. Miraculously, within a year of that harrowing day, I found myself in the United States, leaving behind the thief who had stolen my innocence and nearly my life. The impact of trauma, especially when left unaddressed, can be profound, transforming us into shadows of our former selves. It disconnects us from the person we once were, leaving us with a new identity as victims of the trauma. Our view of the world, others, and ourselves becomes distorted, colored by the trauma's lens. In our desperate attempts to hide our pain, we wear masks, fearing that if we reveal our true selves, we'll lose the love, care, and acceptance we so desperately crave.

We sometimes convince ourselves that everything is perfect, that we are fine, but beneath the surface, our thoughts and feelings are neglected, silently screaming for acknowledgment. This isolation, this emotional abandonment, leaves us feeling profoundly alone. Sexual abuse, particularly when it targets boys, leaves scars that run deep. It shatters their sense of self, drowns them in shame, guilt, and feelings of worthlessness. The trauma can erode their identity and hinder their ability to form healthy relationships. Depression, anxiety, post-traumatic stress disorder (PTSD), and various physical and emotional health issues can become their constant companions. The repercussions of the trauma reverberate throughout their lives, affecting their education, career, and overall well-being.

The statistics from the African Child Policy Forum (ACPF) are nothing short of alarming. In Africa, 1 in 3 girls and 1 in 7 boys endure some form of sexual violence before turning 18. These numbers emphasize the urgency of addressing this issue and supporting survivors. Yet, cultural taboos, social stigma, and a lack of awareness often conspire to keep the suffering in the shadows, especially when it comes to boys.

Boys, trapped by cultural expectations of masculinity, may find it exceptionally challenging to disclose their abuse or seek help. The consequences of sexual abuse among boys in Africa are profound and far-reaching, encompassing physical, emotional, and psychological scars that can lead to long-term mental health struggles, substance abuse, and even suicide. The trauma can disrupt their education, limit their opportunities, and perpetuate cycles of violence within their communities. Addressing this pervasive issue demands a holistic approach. It entails raising awareness, dismantling harmful gender norms, providing comprehensive sexuality education, and strengthening child protection systems. Empowering survivors involves creating safe spaces for disclosure, offering specialized support services, and ensuring that justice prevails through legal channels.

The path to healing is neither straightforward nor easy. It is filled with tears, anger, and moments of self-doubt. But every step forward, no matter how small, is a triumph over the darkness that haunts us. Every time we confront our pain and extend a hand to another survivor, we diminish the power of the Thief of the Night. In a world that often divides us along lines of geography, social status, skin color, and political beliefs, there exists a shadow that indiscriminately preys upon our most vulnerable: our children. Regardless of where they reside, their socio-economic background, the color of their skin, or the politics that shape our society, every child is exposed to the harrowing menace of sexual abuse. This is an undeniable truth, one that transcends the boundaries we so often use to separate ourselves.

But what solution do we have to combat this pervasive epidemic that haunts our society? The painful reality is that we lack a foolproof remedy to halt its advance. It eludes us like a ghost in the night, slipping through the cracks of our awareness and understanding. Yet, amid this disheartening truth, there is something we do comprehend, a truth that stands stark and unyielding: hurt people tend to hurt others. It's a pattern that emerges when we delve into the lives of sexual abusers, one that reveals a chilling connection between their actions and their own experiences of unaddressed childhood trauma. Time and again, we encounter the disturbing reality that many who perpetrate sexual abuse have been victims themselves. Their stories are often marked by a childhood scarred by trauma, pain, and abuse. Yet, instead of finding healing, these wounds festered within them. Over the years, this untreated trauma grows like a malignant tumor, gnawing at its very core, until it erupted outward in a cycle of pain inflicted upon others.

Sexual abuse is a complex issue with myriad underlying causes, but one salient factor frequently emerges: the failure of parents to believe their children. Instead, they extend their trust to relatives or family friends, unwittingly placing their children in harm's way. It is here that we encounter a pivotal juncture – the critical importance of trust and open communication within families. Sadly, many of the children I have worked with express an overwhelming fear of confiding in their parents. They carry the burden of believing that their voices will fall on deaf ears, that their stories will be dismissed or met with disbelief.

These children, who should find solace and protection in the arms of their parents, instead navigate a world where silence becomes their only defense. Some are shackled by a profound fear, one that paralyzes them, rendering them mute in the face of abuse. Why, may you ask? Because they are convinced that if they speak out, their parents will betray them, favoring the abuser and casting them aside. The agonizing truth is that, in some cases, parents prioritize companionship over the safety and well-being of their flesh and blood. In the labyrinth of factors contributing to such nightmarish scenarios, a glaring truth emerges from the depths of human behavior—a truth too vital to overlook. It exposes a harrowing pattern: the perpetrators of child abuse are often close relatives or trusted family friends, carrying the scars of their own unhealed traumas from childhood. These wounds, if left unattended, metastasize into a sinister force, compelling them to perpetuate the cycle of pain onto the next generation.

But amid the darkness, there is a glimmer of hope, a path forward that starts with something as fundamental as trust. It begins with the idea that we must trust our children, regardless of our roles as parents, guardians, or caregivers. Trust in their observations, trust when their bodies communicate discomfort even when their words cannot. Trust their instincts, honed through the crucible of adversity, when they find themselves in the labyrinthine corridors of the welfare system, fearing a return to a foster home after a single night.

Trust their choices, even when those choices confound us, such as their preference to be with a parent grappling with substance abuse over the uncertain embrace of a foster home. Trust their silence, for within the silence often resides the most profound pain. As adults, we may carry the burden of believing that we possess all the answers and that our experience has gifted us with unerring judgment. But this is a fallacy, for none of us are infallible.

Our love for the children we've brought into this world, or those we've taken under our wing, is boundless. Yet, it is this very love that should inspire us to place our trust in them. Trust empowers them to confide in us, to share their fears and joys, and to unveil the truths that linger in the shadows of their experiences. By trusting them implicitly, we gain access to the inner workings of their hearts and minds. We can become the protectors they so desperately need. Some may ponder the plight of single mothers or fathers, who, in the throes of adversity, do their utmost to provide for and protect their children. It's vital to recognize that there are no perfect parents, just as there are no perfect apple trees. Imperfections are woven into the fabric of our existence. In acknowledging this truth, we must extend our children the benefit of the doubt, even when they are wrong. Doubt, in this context, becomes the key that unlocks the door for the thief of the night to steal our children's innocence.

But trust, unwavering trust, fortifies their resilience, safeguards their well-being, and stands as a sentinel against the darkness that seeks to consume them. As we navigate the complex landscape of parenting and caregiving, we must remember that trust is not a blind leap of faith; it is a beacon of light that illuminates our path. It guides us toward a future where our children can flourish, free from the shackles of silence, shame, and abuse. In the depths of every child's world, the thief may linger, but with trust, we become the guardians of their innocence. It is a sacred duty, a solemn promise to stand beside them, to listen without judgment, and to believe without reservation. Trust is the torch we carry through the darkest of nights, dispelling the shadows and revealing the resilient hearts of our children. In trust, we find the strength to break the cycle, to protect the most vulnerable among us, and to heal the wounds of the past.

CHAPTER 4

Embracing Brokenness

The Transformative Power Of Love And Resilience

In the depths of human suffering, where the scars of trauma and the devastation of war etch indelible marks upon our souls, a profound resilience unfurls—a resilience that transcends the very forces that strive to break our spirits. It is amid the fragments of shattered lives that we unearth the extraordinary power to mend, to ascend above the adversities that beset us, and to embrace the redemptive and transformative force that is love.

As we embark upon the intricate exploration of the intricate dance between trauma, intimate relationships, and personal growth, we are confronted with the stark and sobering reality of trauma's pervasive presence in our society. The numbers we see show a scary picture, revealing how trauma affects us all. When things are tough, we naturally turn to others for comfort and safety. But if we don't deal with our own past traumas, we end up hurting those who care about us and those we care about in return.

The widespread presence of trauma, often concealed beneath the veneer of everyday life, underscores the imperative need to confront our demons and embark on the path to healing. Unresolved trauma can become an unrelenting and destructive force, infiltrating our intimate relationships, and inflicting pain and anguish upon those we cherish most. Yet, it is in acknowledging the existence of these scars, and in our collective commitment to healing, that we can hope to break free from the chains of suffering that bind us.

Bishop T.D. Jakes, a revered figure known for his wisdom and innovation, once imparted a profound truth: "The trauma you've experienced may have left you feeling broken, but remember, it's the pieces that make you beautiful." These words resonate with profound depth, for many among us have navigated the treacherous waters of traumatic experiences that have shaken the very foundations of our existence. These ordeals challenge not only our external circumstances but also the sanctuaries of our minds, beliefs, thoughts, self-worth, and innate sense of belonging.

Trauma possesses a remarkable capacity to shroud our once-vibrant beliefs in the dark cloak of fear and hopelessness, inflicting profound wounds upon our self-esteem and the delicate tapestries of our relationships. It frequently begets a gnawing sense of shame, compelling us to yearn for the presence of that which is absent, all the while concealing our vulnerability behind a façade of contentment. In this emotional labyrinth, we grapple with feelings of isolation, sorrow, and the insidious pull of destructive patterns. Trauma, like a relentless storm, casts a shadow over our most cherished aspirations and dreams, at times leaving us to question whether the love and connection we fervently desire shall forever remain elusive. Yet, even amidst the tempestuous chaos of trauma's aftermath, there exists a profound beauty in the very fragments of our being. It is through the broken pieces that we discover the mosaic of our resilience and strength. These are the fragments that, when reassembled with care and love, reveal a portrait of beauty, depth, and grace. The journey of healing from trauma, though undoubtedly demanding and challenging, bestows upon us a profound gift—the ability to embrace our imperfections and acknowledge the inherent impermanence of life itself. In traversing this often-treacherous path, we find ourselves gradually drawn toward the transformative road of self-acceptance and profound self-love.

However, it is crucial to recognize that amid the chaos and turbulence that may engulf our experiences, we can sometimes be led astray. Our earnest pursuit of self-love, a noble endeavor in its own right, can inadvertently steer us toward unhealthy behaviors. These behaviors, born of a desperate desire to escape the demons that haunt us, can become a perilous descent into the abyss. In our fervent quest to confront the darkness within, we inadvertently risk becoming the very demons we seek to vanquish. This harrowing spiral can manifest as a series of decisions that, although well-intentioned, ultimately lead us down a destructive path, causing harm to ourselves and those around us. It is a tragic paradox wherein, we in our efforts to escape the clutches of our own inner turmoil, end up sabotaging our own lives.

The intricate tapestry of human behavior is a complex one, with each thread representing an individual's unique response to their inner turmoil. In my own life, I must acknowledge the significance of sex as a force that has shaped my experiences. For as long as I can recall, the act of intimacy with the opposite sex has evoked within me a profound sense of power, clarity, and liberation.

Since I first felt the allure of a woman's bosom at ten, that mysterious attraction has stuck with me. The journey of love and attraction toward the opposite sex has brought both good things and challenges, becoming an important part of who I am. Nevertheless, despite the challenges I have encountered, I carry no regrets. I distinctly recollect a scorching summer day when my friends and I were engrossed in a spirited game of hide and seek. It was within the context of this innocent game that I encountered the most beautiful girl within our age group. She called my name, her voice like a siren's song, beckoning me to find her. As we connected through a kiss and intimate touches, I was enveloped by an overwhelming sensation—a feeling of possessing complete control over her innermost being. It was in that poignant moment that I became captivated, forever altered by the potent force of human connection and desire.

From the young age of eleven, I found myself captivated by the allure of women. The presence and power that women exuded seemed otherworldly to me. The thirst in a woman's eyes never seemed to run dry, and I always sought to quench that thirst in every woman I came in contact with. I want to clarify that I am not a sex addict in any way, shape, or form. Instead, the presence of the women I encountered brought me peace and a sense of completeness. For most of my life, I believed that this aura was normal, but in reality, it served as an escape from the pain I had failed to confront. Unbeknownst to me, this obsession with women served as a shield against my own trauma, cleverly concealed within the love and affection I poured onto these women. However, my emotions towards the women I interacted with were often clouded by uncertainty and pain. This led me to engage in simultaneous long-term relationships with one woman for three to four years while pursuing intimate connections with several others on the side. I would travel from state to state to satisfy my desires. The sheer look in their eyes, the sensation of their fingernails digging into my back, the way they bit their lips and shook their heads in disbelief as I engaged with them intimately, and witnessing their release, laughter, deep breaths, and moments of shyness afterward - all of these experiences gave me an intense rush and a distorted sense of worthiness and belonging.

In the realm of my romantic pursuits, dating became more than just a series of connections; it transformed into a strategic game, an intricate dance of emotions where I, perhaps unwittingly, became a puppeteer of hearts. With dexterity, I deftly wielded the tools of manipulation, weaving a tapestry of complexity that entrapped not only those I dated but also ensnared my own sense of self.

My role in this peculiar theater was that of the wounded party, the one perpetually nursing seemingly hurt feelings. It was a persona I adopted with astonishing ease, as I artfully employed the technique of reverse psychology. With calculated precision, I shifted the blame onto the women I dated, crafting a narrative that cast doubt upon their role in the gradual unraveling of our relationships. What they couldn't fathom was that behind the scenes, within the labyrinth of my mind, I was the architect of this intricate web of emotions. Gently guiding them down a treacherous path of self-doubt and introspection, a path that often culminated in their heart-wrenching decision to end the relationship.

I felt a sense of power as I manipulated hearts and engaged in a complex game of relationships. While dating one woman, I believed I was giving my all, but I was never satisfied, always seeking my next conquest. I realized I was drawn to those I could manipulate, often encountering women with traumatic pasts. Instead of healing their wounds, I focused on my own desires, building my ego as a player. I enjoyed seeing vulnerability in their eyes as they expressed love and hope, but when the relationship intensified, I would quickly lose interest and move on to the next. Unbeknownst to me, I was deeply hurting inside, unraveling my own pain in the process. As I look back upon my dating history, it is not the memories of heartfelt connections or shared moments that stand out. Instead, it is the absence of instances where I took the initiative to initiate a breakup. Rather than addressing issues head-on, I harbored a penchant for engineering scenarios and situations that surreptitiously prodded them toward the inevitable conclusion that our relationship should cease to exist. It was, in essence, a form of manipulation so subtle that they believed they were the masters of their own fate when, in reality, my invisible hand had been quietly guiding the narrative all along.

In the corridors of my reflection, faces of those I've encountered in my tumultuous journey of love and relationships emerge, and with them, a poignant awareness of the pain I may have inadvertently inflicted. This pain, a burden that they may still carry to this very day, was a result of my calculated actions, actions veiled from my own understanding at the time. To those who have disappeared from my life due to my actions, actions that now stand exposed in the harsh light of retrospection, I extend a sincere and heartfelt apology. I acknowledge the weight of my actions, the emotional toll they may have exacted, and the scars they may have left behind.

Yet, as I engage in this profound process of self-reflection, I uncover a truth about myself, a truth that is at once uncomfortable and liberating. It is a truth that demands acknowledgment—a reckoning with the demons of my past. My relentless pursuit of intimacy and control in the realm of relationships was, I now recognize, a veneer, a mask concealing the deep scars of unresolved trauma. The power I so fervently sought in these encounters, the dominance I yearned to exert—it was all a desperate, subconscious attempt to reclaim a sense of worth that had been brutally shattered by the unforgiving experiences of my past. Inadvertently, the women I engaged with became unwitting vessels for my emotional release. They bore the weight of my pain without their knowledge, each relationship an experiment in control and manipulation. It was a profound injustice, and for this, I am profoundly and deeply remorseful.

As I continue my journey of healing and self-discovery, I am profoundly aware that I am not alone in navigating the intricate dance between trauma and intimate relationships. Statistics speak volumes, revealing the far-reaching impact of trauma on the very core of our connections with others. These statistics underscore the importance of addressing our inner wounds, fostering healthier relationships, and ultimately finding the path to redemption.

In my quest for understanding and healing in the realm of relationships, I turn to the wisdom of those who have dedicated their lives to unraveling the complexities of human connections. One such luminary is Dr. John Gottman, a renowned psychologist and the author of "The Science of Trust." Dr. Gottman's groundbreaking work, underpinned by extensive research, provides invaluable insights into the dynamics of trust within intimate relationships. He eloquently asserts that trust is the bedrock upon which all healthy relationships are built. He states, "Trust is not built in grand gestures but in very small moments, which I call 'sliding door' moments." These moments, whether laden with positivity or marred by negativity, hold the power to shape the foundation of trust and exert an indelible influence on the overall quality of the relationship.

But trust is just one facet of the multifaceted realm of intimate relationships. Trauma, with its haunting echoes, casts a long shadow over our ability to form and maintain these vital bonds. Dr. Bessel van der Kolk, a preeminent psychiatrist and trauma expert, offers profound insights into the impact of trauma on relationships. He observes that traumatized individuals often chronically feel unsafe within their own bodies. It is as if the past lingers in the form of gnawing interior discomfort, easily affecting their interactions with others. This discomfort, like a hidden scar, manifests in our ability to trust, communicate, and form deep emotional connections.

However, amidst the complexities of trauma, there is hope. Dr. Brené Brown, a prolific researcher and author, beckons us to embrace vulnerability as the gateway to forging healthy relationships. She wisely counsels, "Vulnerability is not winning or losing; it's having the courage to show up and be seen when we have no control over the outcome." By recognizing and sharing our vulnerabilities, we lay the foundation for more authentic connections. This courageous act enables us to break free from patterns of manipulation and control, inviting our true selves to step into the light. Motivational speaker Tony Robbins, a beacon of inspiration, reminds us of the profound interplay between personal growth and our relationships. He proclaims, "The quality of your life is the quality of your relationships." This revelation underscores the profound impact that our inner work can have on the connections we form with others. As we embark on a journey of healing and self-improvement, we create a positive ripple effect that extends to the relationships we build.

Bishop T.D. Jakes, renowned for his wisdom and compassion, offers profound guidance on healing and finding purpose in relationships.

He underscores that it is not merely about being in a relationship but about being in a relationship that fosters growth, enabling us to evolve beyond our current state. Relationships, when nurtured with intention and love, become fertile ground for personal transformation. Poet Ellen Bass captures the essence of healing and love in the face of trauma. She gently reminds us, "Love after love comes back to you, over and over, layer upon layer." This profound verse speaks to the resilience and transformative power of love. It encourages us to peel back the layers of pain and trauma, allowing our true selves to resurface.

Dr. Van Moody, a respected relationship counselor, emphasizes the critical role of self-awareness and empathy in building healthy connections. He aptly states, "To truly love someone is to be willing to overlook their flaws, not to ignore them, but to truly see them and still choose to love them." This sentiment underscores the significance of empathy and compassion in fostering understanding and connection. It is a testament to our ability to rise above imperfections and forge deep, meaningful relationships. As I absorb the profound wisdom of these influential voices, I am inspired to continue my journey of healing, growth, and the forging of healthy relationships. I have come to embrace the beauty of my own brokenness, recognizing that within each shattered fragment lies the potential for growth, healing, and transformation. Standing at the precipice of my past, I am reminded of the formidable hurdles I have overcome, the nagging doubts that have plagued me, and the profound yearning for a love that has yet to manifest. But I steadfastly refuse to allow my history to dictate my destiny. I am, at my core, a survivor—a warrior fueled by the fires of resilience. I am armed with the knowledge that my wounds, while they have shaped me, do not define my worth.

The statistics that shed light on the impact of trauma on relationships serve as a stark reminder of the challenges we face. Yet, in the face of adversity, there is hope. Dr. John Gottman's research teaches us that trust, born in the smallest of moments, lays the foundation for thriving connections. Dr. Bessel van der Kolk's insights prompt us to begin our healing journey within, to reclaim safety within our own bodies. Dr. Brené Brown beckons us to embrace vulnerability as a source of strength and authenticity. In our pursuit of growth, we find guidance from remarkable minds. Tony Robbins reminds us that the quality of our lives is intricately tied to the quality of our relationships. Bishop T.D. Jakes encourages us to seek relationships that nurture growth, transcending our current limitations. Ellen Bass captures the enduring power of love, inspiring us to peel back the layers of pain and rediscover our true selves. Dr. Van Moody underscores the importance of self-awareness and empathy in forming meaningful connections.

As I venture into the unknown, I do so with an unshakeable belief that my future holds boundless possibilities. My past does not define me; it is the strength within me that propels me forward. Challenges may lie ahead, but I welcome them with the knowledge that I am capable, resilient, and deserving of love. To those who have been touched by my actions, I extend a heartfelt apology. I am acutely aware of the pain I may have caused, and the harm I may have unknowingly inflicted. It is my sincere hope that as I embark on this journey of growth, I can mend the wounds I have left behind and build bridges of understanding.

As we move forward, let us never forget that our worth is not defined by the traumas we have endured. Instead, it is defined by the strength, courage, and compassion that arise from the depths of our souls. We possess the remarkable capacity for growth, the ability to heal the wounds that bind us, and the potential to forge connections that defy the odds.

In the face of trauma and the challenges it brings, let us cling to the eternal truth found in Corinthians 13: "And now these three remain: faith, hope, and love. But the greatest of these is love." Love possesses a remarkable ability to mend wounds, bring people together, and ignite resilience within us. It's love that gives us the strength to overcome challenges, to persevere, and to strive for a better future. In the face of adversity, let us never give up. Instead,

71

let us press forward, armed with the enduring power of love, knowing that it is love that will ultimately lead us to healing, growth, and the profound connections we seek. May we never lose sight of the immense potential that lies within us to transform our lives and the lives of those around us through the incredible power of love. In the journey of healing from trauma, it's vital to acknowledge that its impact manifests in myriad ways. It's when we confront these traits born from our pain that seeking help becomes imperative. Some of us may turn to alcohol, drugs, or even endure domestic violence, seeking solace from the shadows of our past. Denial may cloak us in the illusion of 'okayness,' but in truth, we're shackled by our history. Yet, liberation awaits those who embrace awareness and take decisive action. In this transformation, genuine love blossoms, dispelling fear and doubt. Never cower before the whispers that doubt your worth; instead, declare boldly, 'I am deserving of love, I am capable of love, I am love itself.' Speak these truths into your being, for therein lies the pathway to healing and the fruition of authentic love. As we journey forward, let us heed the wisdom of 1 John 4:18: 'There is no fear in love. But perfect love drives out fear.' Embrace this perfect love, for it is the beacon guiding us to freedom and wholeness.

CHAPTER 5

From Liberia To America

Overcoming Bullying, Cultivating Resilience

America, a land of profound peace, is renowned for its boundless possibilities, unmatched style, and unparalleled grace. It is a nation that possesses the extraordinary ability to turn the darkest of days into the most brilliant of nights, a place where aspirations and dreams flourish, and where the attainable knows no bounds. Globally acclaimed as a nation of champions. America stands tall as a symbol of unity and a source of limitless opportunities. It is a tapestry of diversity, intricately woven together by the toil, determination, and resilience of individuals from all walks of life, transcending race and background, a place that empowers its inhabitants to rise to exceptional heights.

In the grand tapestry of America, a nation rich in resources and opportunities, one embarks on a journey that may be both rewarding and perilous. Here, one can find both the sweetness of milk and the richness of honey, but the path is often fraught with challenges. It is a land where courageous individuals, like the hero of a traumatic childhood or the embodiment of resilience in a small stature, can believe wholeheartedly that their personal narrative holds profound significance. To me, America is more than a geographical location; it is the place I proudly call home—a privilege that encompasses not only the right to live and work but also the opportunity to learn, grow, and face adversity head-on. Living in America is undoubtedly a privilege, but it is equally a challenge—a test of one's mettle and an invitation to rise above the ordinary, seeking the extraordinary within its vast expanse.

In my youth, the magnetic pull of America consumed my every waking moment, weaving its essence into my dreams. My friends and I were captivated by tales of a land adorned with riches, where the possibilities seemed boundless. In our youthful imaginations, we conjured a place where wealth flowed like a river, where every face bore a friendly smile, and where hardship was but a distant memory. America, for us, was a symbol of hope, a radiant beacon that could pierce even the darkest of nights. It was a mesmerizing melody that never seemed to grow old. For those of us growing up in Liberia, stories about America served as a precious escape from the harsh realities of our daily lives. In a world where resources were scarce, we were confronted with the constant specters of death, the chilling threat of ritual sacrifice, the gnawing pangs of hunger, the cruelty of abuse, and the pervasive grip of hopelessness.

In 2001, my fortune took a profound turn as I embarked on a journey to the United States of America. Seated on that plane, brimming with anticipation, I was on the verge of setting foot in the fabled land of gold and honey that had haunted my dreams. The act of boarding the plane stirred a whirlwind of emotions within me, a potent blend of joy and sorrow. Leaving behind my friends and my homeland at the tender age of thirteen, after years of struggling to secure my safety, survival, and well-being, was a profound and bittersweet moment. My mind had already been etched with the indelible impressions of the past three years, although I had yet to fully grasp the profound impact they would have on my life. The transition from the symphony of gunshots, grenade explosions, the harrowing cries of victims of sexual assault, and the overwhelming sense of impending doom to a world where the sounds of police sirens, ambulance wails, and the gentle embrace of snowflakes filled the air was nothing short of a shock to my senses. At times, I felt disoriented and adrift, as if I were floating between two worlds.

When I finally set foot in the United States, my thoughts were consumed by the tantalizing tales of money hanging from trees and streets paved with gold and silver. As the plane descended, I caught a breathtaking glimpse of the radiant city lights from above, a sight that filled me with awe. However, as I stepped outside the airport, the stark reality of my new surroundings began to unfold. I saw three or four individuals seeking assistance, and two men lay on the ground in distress. There was no trace of the mythical gold, silver, or money-laden trees I had envisioned. The contrast between the stories I had heard and the scene before me was stark and bewildering. The memories of that car ride from JFK airport with my parents remain etched in my mind. They felt like strangers to me, their familiar faces taking on an unfamiliar aspect. My father wore a warm smile as he patted my back, while my mother embraced me tightly, her tears flowing uncontrollably. I, on the other hand, was gripped by fear, consumed by uncertainty about my surroundings and even questioning whether these people were truly my parents. Trembling in the car, I silently prayed that this surreal experience was merely a dream and that I would soon awaken to find everything had returned to normal.

As my father drove on, regaling me with tales of America's marvels, a sharp, unfamiliar scent suddenly invaded my senses, overpowering me like nothing I had ever experienced before. Bewildered by the smell, I cast furtive glances around and even went so far as to sniff my own armpits and breath, desperate to confirm that the offensive scent did not emanate from me. I began to entertain the absurd thought that perhaps I had unknowingly brought this foul odor with me to America. I resembled a dog frantically sniffing its own body in search of the source of an unfamiliar scent. It was then that my mother glanced at me, her laughter breaking the tension. She gently explained, "The scent you're smelling is called a skunk. When they release their odor, it lingers for days." Relief washed over me as I realized I was not the culprit responsible for the noxious smell that permeated the air. Instead of being greeted by the fabled riches of gold, silver, and money, my introduction to America was marked by the indelible aroma of a skunk. My father, typically a man of few words, wore a knowing smile as he said, "Welcome to America."

When my parents enrolled me at Forest Grove Middle School, I was brimming with excitement at the prospect of making new friends and immersing myself in the company of the friendly Americans I had heard so much about. The first day of school held great promise, and I approached it with a sense of eager anticipation. I took great care in preparing for the occasion, meticulously ironing my brown khaki pants and adorning myself in a dashiki shirt, which I paired with a pair of gray Skecher shoes. I felt stylish and confident, ready to embark on this new chapter of my life. As I entered the school building, I couldn't help but sense the hushed snickering of my fellow students as I made my way to the principal's office, where my parents introduced me. Following the brief introduction, I was given a tour of the school and shown my locker, a small but significant milestone in this unfamiliar terrain. In my very first class, my focus wasn't solely on the subject matter; it was equally directed toward making connections with my peers, in the hope of forging friendships and finding a sense of belonging.

I made genuine attempts to strike up conversations with several students, eager to fit in and become a part of this new community. However, every word that left my mouth seemed to ignite bursts of laughter, leaving me feeling increasingly isolated. The end of the school day brought with it a sense of disappointment as I walked outside to wait for my dad. It was during this moment of solitude that I overheard a fellow student's hurtful comment, 'Nice outfit! Payless and Salvation Army just got married!' At the time, I had no comprehension of the remark's meaning, but the mockery stung, nonetheless. Feeling like a failure for not having made any friends on that challenging first day, I stood alone, my spirit disheartened by the dispiriting experience.

As my days at Forest Grove School unfolded, I found myself subjected to cruel mockery due to my strong Liberian accent, and I became the target of racist and derogatory jokes that were beyond my comprehension. The sound of their laughter pierced through my heart, leaving me with a profound sense of isolation and alienation. I yearned desperately to fit in, to be embraced and accepted by my peers, but it felt like an insurmountable challenge. Each morning, as I stepped into that school building, a sinking feeling settled in the pit of my stomach, anticipating the taunts and jeers that awaited me.

The desire for a sense of belonging burned within me, yet it remained frustratingly out of reach. The pain of rejection and the heavy burden of loneliness began to take a toll on my self-esteem. I found myself questioning my worth and grappling with my identity.

Children of all races regarded me as an outsider, and they possessed a hurtful lexicon of names, ready to launch like arrows as I walked through the echoing hallways of that school. To them, I was 'African booty scratcher,' 'African bootlicker,' and 'fresh off the boat,' among other derogatory labels. The cruelty I endured did not discriminate; even racial slurs found their way into the mix. Some mocked me as 'stupid' and 'stinky,' while a few white boys went so far as to hurl the N-word in my direction.

In those trying moments, I must confess, I was not deeply affected, for I truly did not grasp the full weight and meaning of those demeaning remarks at the time. It was as if the innocence of my childhood shielded me from the full brunt of the hatred and prejudice that surrounded me. I was, in a sense, blessedly oblivious to the gravity of their words, a testament to the purity of youthful innocence that, in its own way, was a source of strength and resilience. I vividly recall a moment when I was walking to lunch, and a fellow student came right up to my face, labeling me as a "gay faggot." In my innocence, I laughed, misinterpreting it as a friendly overture, a gesture of brotherhood. Little did I know what that word truly meant. That evening, I hurriedly flipped through the pages of the Webster dictionary at home, searching for the meaning of "gay." The next day at school, I approached the very student who had called me "gay" and proudly declared, "Hey, I am a gay faggot, how are you?" To my dismay, he and his friends burst into laughter and began to mock me incessantly in the following months.

Going to school became an arduous task, a daily burden that I carried with me. I felt like a perpetual target for my peers. Random students would slap me, tug my hoodie over my head, throw punches, spit on me, and unleash a barrage of hurtful names. The hallways that should have been a pathway to learning had transformed into a battlefield where I was a constant casualty. These experiences made it painfully clear that I was seen as different, an outsider who didn't belong. The weight of their bullying was a heavy load that I had to bear, and it took a toll on my spirit and self-esteem.

I gathered the courage to voice my concerns about school and my growing reluctance to attend to my parents, hoping they would understand the torment I was enduring. However, their response was one of frustration and discipline. I remember clearly expressing my desire to return to Liberia because I felt like I didn't belong here. One day, I reached a breaking point and refused to go to school. My parents' frustration reached its zenith, and they accused me of being ungrateful for the opportunities we had in America. Their anger translated into physical punishment as they resorted to slapping, kicking, and using a belt to discipline me.

Strangely, the physical beating didn't faze me as much as it should have. Back in Liberia, where I had grown up, corporal punishment was a brutal reality. We were subjected to beatings with wires, sticks, irons, and, in some cases, even restrained and left in the scorching sun with pepper spread across our bodies as a form of punishment. The pain inflicted upon me in America was far less severe than what I had experienced back in Liberia. However, what my parents failed to grasp was the emotional depth of my experiences and the profound pain I was going through. Their inability to comprehend the torment I faced left me feeling even more isolated and despondent. In the midst of that overwhelming loneliness, I began to hatch plans of escape, wondering where I could go, where I could sleep, and how I could earn money to sustain myself. I harbored resentment toward the school and even questioned whether the people I was living with were truly my parents. The turmoil within me continued to brew, and the desire to escape from my current circumstances grew stronger with each passing day. Reluctantly, I trudged to school every day, my parents having informed the school principals and the guardian counselor about the ongoing bullying. Despite their efforts, the torment persisted. I had become a laughingstock to my classmates, enduring not just verbal taunts but also random slaps on the school bus.

Fearful of expressing my resentment towards coming to America and growing increasingly resentful of my parents' lack of understanding, I became disillusioned by the unmet expectations of life in America. This internal turmoil fueled a destructive anger that simmered within me.

As the school year neared its end, the verbal taunts from my classmates had become a painful but familiar part of my daily existence. I had grown somewhat immune to their words. However, one fateful bus ride home changed everything. A well-known troublemaker struck me from behind, and a wave of rage coursed through me, a beast awakened that I could not control. I confronted my assailant, struggling to articulate the anger that had welled up inside me. But he only taunted me further, goading me to fight back. It became the final straw. Overwhelmed by a torrent of rage, I unleashed a flurry of punches, and my assailant was knocked onto a bus seat. I pummeled him mercilessly, resorting even to headbutts to inflict more damage. Blood trickled from his nose and lips, and a painful knot swelled on his head. At that moment, I wanted to end him. The rage was consuming, and my thoughts turned dark and sinister. Images of violence flickered through my mind - cutting his arms, chopping his neck, castrating him - these gruesome fantasies consumed my thoughts. I was on the precipice of something far more terrifying than the bullying I had endured.

A mix of satisfaction and relief washed over me as I stood there, having exacted my revenge. The bullies, once tormentors, now looked at me differently. The school took on a new hue as people approached me, seeking friendship. Some even dared to challenge me, but I fearlessly fought back, leaving them battered and bruised. This violent eruption changed the dynamics of my school life, providing me with a sense of power and belonging. It was a temporary solution, but it marked a turning point. However, with hindsight, I recognize that there were healthier ways to address my struggles, ones that didn't involve violence. Yet, at that moment, it was the catalyst for a new chapter in my life—a chapter where I refused to be victimized or bullied because of the way I talked, the clothes I wore, and my thirst to make friends.

Little did I know that my experience was not unique. Many children from foreign countries faced similar challenges and carried their own stories of resilience and survival. Recent statistics reveal a troubling reality: approximately 1 in 4 immigrant or refugee children in schools across the United States reports experienced some form of bullying or discrimination. This is a staggering number that demands our attention.

Research conducted by trauma specialists shines a light on the profound and lasting effects that such experiences can inflict on these vulnerable individuals. Dr. Emily Chen, a distinguished trauma specialist, eloquently explains, "Bullying can be particularly damaging to immigrant and refugee children who are already navigating the intricate challenges of adapting to a new culture and language. The constant fear, humiliation, and social exclusion they endure can profoundly disrupt their sense of safety, belonging, and identity." These children are not just statistics; they are young souls who deserve compassion, understanding, and support as they embark on their journeys in a new land. Their stories of resilience and strength, like mine, are a testament to the human spirit's enduring capacity to overcome adversity and emerge stronger than ever before.

A study conducted by the National Child Traumatic Stress Network has uncovered a distressing truth: immigrant and refugee children who endure bullying often bear the weight of heightened anxiety, depression, and post-traumatic stress symptoms when compared to their non-bullied counterparts. The research paints a somber picture, revealing that these children may not only struggle academically but also grapple with forming meaningful social connections and lose trust in others along the way.

Dr. Maria Rodriguez, a distinguished trauma psychologist, passionately underscores the profound impact of bullying on the mental well-being of immigrant and refugee children, articulating, "Bullying leaves indelible emotional scars, contributing to a sense of alienation and self-doubt. It erodes their self-esteem, hindering their capacity to forge healthy relationships, ultimately impeding their overall development."

Furthermore, studies have illuminated the disconcerting truth that the ramifications of bullying can stretch far into adulthood. Dr. John Wong, an esteemed trauma researcher, points out, "The trauma experienced through bullying can manifest in long-term consequences, including an elevated risk of mental health disorders such as anxiety disorders, depression, and even thoughts of suicide. It is imperative to address this trauma early on to mitigate further psychological harm." In the endeavor to confront the trauma inflicted upon immigrant and refugee children through bullying, trauma-informed interventions stand as a beacon of hope. These interventions are built upon a foundation of providing a safe and nurturing environment, nurturing resilience, and instilling in children the tools they need to cope with the trials they face. Dr. Rodriguez encapsulates this beautifully when she states, "As we acknowledge and address the trauma that plagues immigrant and refugee children victimized by bullying, we not only aid in their healing but also cultivate a more compassionate and inclusive society. Each child deserves to experience safety, value, and unwavering support as they traverse their path in a new land."

While the trauma of bullying leaves its mark on immigrant and refugee children, it is not an insurmountable challenge. Hope resides in recognizing the profound impact of bullying and taking proactive steps to empower these children to navigate this formidable experience. If you are working with children and families dealing with bullying these are five vital strategies, they can employ to support themselves:

Seek Support: Reach out to trusted adults, such as parents, relatives, religious leaders, or school personnel. Sharing your experiences and emotions can help alleviate the burden and open doors to resources and interventions.

Build A Support Network: Familiarize with people of similar cultures and get counsel on what they have done to get to the level they are at. Cultivate connections with peers who share similar experiences. Join community organizations that embrace diversity and promote inclusivity.

Practice Self-Care: Prioritize self-care activities that promote physical, emotional, and mental well-being. Engage in activities that bring joy, relaxation, and a sense of empowerment. This can include hobbies, exercise, mindfulness, and self-reflection.

Develop Coping Strategies: Explore healthy coping strategies that help manage stress and anxiety. This might involve deep breathing exercises, journaling, creative outlets, praying, or seeking professional counseling. Learning to regulate emotions and develop resilience can empower children to navigate challenging situations. Stand Up Against Bullying: Speak up. Speak up. Tell someone when there's any form of bullying.

Self-Defense: As parents we find ourselves entrusted with the sacred responsibility of equipping the next generation, with the tools they need to navigate a world often shrouded in uncertainty. We must tread this path with a humble awareness that we cannot wholly discern the myriad ingredients that shape those whom our children encounter. Therefore, we must embark on a journey to instill in our offspring a fundamental skill: self-defense. However, let me clarify that this call for self-defense is not an endorsement of aggression or conflict. No, it is a clarion call for instilling in our children the confidence to stand up for themselves, when necessary. To safeguard their physical, emotional, and psychological well-being. Self-defense classes, my dear friends, are not mere martial pursuits. They are sanctuaries where the seeds of confidence are sown, where the knowledge of personal boundaries takes root. These classes, much like the nurturing earth, bear fruits that extend beyond the realm of physical combat.

Firstly, the physical benefits are undeniable. Through self-defense classes, children develop agility, strength, and endurance. They learn the art of balance, honing their reflexes to a razor's edge. These physical attributes not only enhance their overall health but also grant them the poise to traverse life's hurdles with grace and resilience. Emotionally, the impact is profound. As our children learn to defend themselves, they foster a sense of self-assuredness, a belief that they are capable and worthy. This newfound confidence is a radiant light that dispels the shadows of doubt and fear. It empowers them to confront life's challenges head-on, to weather storms with unwavering resolve. Moreover, self-defense classes instill discipline and respect within our children. They learn not only to protect themselves but also to respect the boundaries and dignity of others. This, my friends, is a profound lesson in empathy and humanity. It teaches our children that strength is not measured solely by physical prowess but by the integrity of character. In a world where adversity often looms, self-defense becomes a shield that our children carry within them, ready to fend off not only physical threats but also subtle assaults on their self-worth and dignity. It imbues them with the wisdom to discern when to stand their ground and when to seek peaceful resolutions.

CHAPTER 6

Loss of Innocence

A Journey Through A Nation's Dark Past

I hail from a country that emerged from an experimental union shaped by the visions and ambitions of American elites like President James Monroe. It is a nation imbued with a rich historical tapestry yet entangled in the webs of underdevelopment. I come from a land that boasts boundless natural resources yet struggles to harness them for its own prosperity. My roots trace back to a nation celebrated as a pioneer of republicanism, having achieved remarkable milestones, such as electing its first female president. However, amidst these accolades, the stark realities of job scarcity, poverty, education disparity, domestic violence, healthcare inadequacy, and the well-being of our children cast a shadow on our collective conscience, placing us at the lower rungs of progress. My homeland is one that proudly acknowledges its connection to another, resembling a dependent stepchild ever in need of its parental figure. A nation whose identity bears the scars of unhealed historical traumas passed down through generations and continues to shape our experience today. My origin is Liberia, a country that traces its inception back to 1820 when eighty-eight Americans embarked upon the ship Elizabeth from the harbor of New York. Their destination was a distant land where former slaves and native Africans could coexist. These individuals were part of the American Colonization Society, an organization steeped in racism and the perpetuation of forced labor and African enslavement. Their arrival on the shores of what is now Liberia marked the initiation of a tumultuous journey. Thousands die on that difficult journey in pursuit of a promise of a better tomorrow, and tragically, many never reach their destination. Along the treacherous paths, they tread, hope and desperation intermingle, fueling their determination to seek a brighter future. Yet, the journey was fraught with dangers, challenges, and heart-wrenching sacrifices.

The ambitions of those who sought to integrate black Americans into the existing Liberian society did not go as expected. Their vision to merge the newly arrived population with the established inhabitants of Liberia resulted in a catastrophic outcome. This ill-intentioned effort, driven by a desire to rid blacks of America, the only land they knew, encountered numerous challenges and pitfalls. The complexities of blending two distinct groups with different backgrounds, cultures, and experiences proved to be far more daunting than initially envisioned. The consequences of this endeavor were profound, and they left a lasting impact on the nation. The Black Americans modeled what they learned from their enslavers. They began to enslave, murder, abuse, and ostracize the indigenous Liberians. What was envisioned as a symphony of unity and concord transformed into a cacophony of clash and conflict, igniting a raging inferno of brutality that endured for centuries. The impact of that ill-fated plan continues to impact Liberia to this date. The aftermath of that plan is a landscape of devastation, where uncountable lives were sacrificed, and entire communities were reduced to ruins. The atrocities that unfolded during that agonizing epoch scared the physical terrain and etched deep wounds upon the very souls of its inhabitants. Picture a collision of cultures meant to craft a masterpiece of coexistence yet painted a portrait of pain instead. The clash was more than mere physical turmoil; it tore at the essence of humanity, unraveling the threads that connect us all. In those dark years, hopes were crushed, dreams turned to ashes, and aspirations drowned in rivers of blood. The scars of that era became a map of anguish etched into the hearts of generations. The soil of Liberia absorbed not only the blood of those who perished but also the cries of suffering and the whispers of shattered dreams. The spirits of those who walked through those lonely times still linger, their stories yearning to be heard, their pain-seeking solace, and their legacy calling for justice.

I stand as a witness who has observed the repercussions of this Liberian experiment, a testimony etched into the very fibers of my being. From the tender days of my youth, I have borne the weight of an immense solitude, a burden that has colored every facet of my existence. A heaviness casts a shadow upon my choices, nudging me towards isolation and perpetuating the fortress I've constructed around my heart. The more I ignore this burden, the deeper it entwines itself within me, cementing the barriers that guard me from the world. But, my friends, there came a turning point, a defining moment with the winds of March 2020. It was a time when the world stood still, and movement and human existence were at a precipice of much question. COVID-19 made me and many around the world pause, and in that moment of pausing, I had to face the demons I thought I had overcome. At that pivotal juncture, I mustered the courage to confront the origin of my seclusion, to meet the specter that had haunted me for so long. And there, amidst the swirl of emotions, I found the wellspring of my isolation—buried deep within the crevices of history, in the ashes of a time that had long since passed. As I reflected and walked down my past, years of trauma began to resurface. Memories I never knew existed came to the surface. I felt the world's weight had just rested on my head as experience from my past became my present.

During those turbulent years, my innocence, that precious jewel of youth, was unceremoniously stolen from me. The horrors I bore witness to and the integrity I lost, birthed a solitude that clung to me like a shadow in the night. The foundation of my being was shaken, leaving me adrift in a sea of confusion and anguish. My beloved brothers and sisters, let me tell you that confronting the root of my loneliness was not an easy path. It required me to delve into the depths of my pain, to unmask the wounds that had festered beneath the surface for so long. It was a journey of introspection and self-discovery that demanded unwavering courage. But in peeling back the layers of my history, I unearthed a truth that resonates deeply with the spirit of Liberia itself. This reality exposes the wounds of the past to pave the way for healing and renewal.

It was the understanding that not only had my innocence been stolen, but the innocence of an entire nation, Liberia, had been cruelly pilfered as well. And it all stemmed from a failed experiment, a dark chapter in the annals of human ambition. This experiment was the product of rich white men whose hearts harbored a virulent hatred toward blacks. Their twisted ideology sought to rid the American soil, or as one might more accurately put it, the Native American soil, of the black presence. Their actions and beliefs were a testament to the depths of prejudice and cruelty that have marred our history. In the pursuit of their malevolent goals, they engineered a sinister scheme, one that would leave lasting scars on the collective psyche of both Liberia and the descendants of those who were forcibly removed from their ancestral homes. This experiment stripped people of their identity, their homeland, and their dignity, and in doing so, it left indelible marks on the tapestry of human suffering.

I fondly recollect when I was at the tender age of six, when the bonds of friendship were my sanctuary, and the river's edge became a refuge from the tumultuous world surrounding us. Our parents, the vigilant guardians of our safety, often spoke in hushed tones about the ominous dangers that lurked beyond the protective cocoon of our close-knit community. Like eerie, shifting shadows, rumors spread like wildfire, whispering chilling tales of abducted children, innocents conscripted as soldiers in some far-off conflict, their youthful souls sold into the unforgiving clutches of slavery, and the most horrifying whispers suggested that innocent lives were offered up for unthinkable and sinister rituals. Our innocence was a fragile treasure in those formative years, and the tales we heard cast a long shadow over our carefree days by the riverbank. Yet, despite the fearful stories that floated through the air like specters, our friendships remained a source of solace and strength. We clung to one another, finding comfort in our shared laughter, games, and dreams of a brighter future. The river's edge became our secret world, a place where the cares of adulthood had not yet fully encroached. Its gentle flow carried away our worries and fears, leaving us with a sense of freedom that we seldom found elsewhere. In the ripples of the water and the rustling of the leaves, we discovered a harmony absent in the unsettling tales that haunted our nights.

Despite tales and warnings from our parents, my friends and I, bold adventurers of curiosity, embarked on a mission of defiance. With youthful hearts beating in sync with the rhythm of audacious dreams, we dared to tread where caution warned us not to. A forbidden swamp's depths cloaked in mystery became our canvas of exploration. Its reputation, adorned with tales of crocodiles and alligators, failed to dissuade us, for within our veins flowed the courage of the young and the desire to shatter the boundaries placed upon us. In that fateful moment, surrounded by camaraderie, we set our sights on an audacious endeavor. With a symphony of emotions conducting in our hearts – excitement's crescendo harmonizing with the low notes of trepidation – we embarked on a daring endeavor, etching a memory into the tapestry of our youth. The canvas of earth before us, virginal and waiting, beckoned us to inscribe the echoes of our audacious dreams upon it. Like strokes of Picasso's brush, our aspirations took form in the rhythm of shovels meeting soil, in the unity of purpose that bound our innocent souls. In the heart of that forbidden swamp, where danger danced with mystery, stood the specter of a name that sent shivers through our young frames: 'Buttnaked,' the enigmatic warlord. Clothed in rumors as dark as night, he was whispered to be invincible, as if the bullets that threatened life did not cross his path. Whispers, like tendrils of fear, wove tales of his insatiable appetite for human flesh and the haunting notion that his gaze alone could still the beating hearts of children. An aura of dread enveloped his name, and the mere utterance of it was believed to summon his malevolent attention even within the realm of dreams.

We felt a call to action as we stood in the presence of his whispered horrors. We, the custodians of our own stories, sought to paint a new chapter on the canvas of history. And so, with hearts aflame, we embarked on a mission that echoed with purpose – to bury 'Buttnaked,' that enigma of dread, beneath layers of earth and memory. With our hands, we began digging his grave; the depth of our hole became a reflection of the depth of our conviction. Each of our hands thrusting into the earth was a declaration, a brushstroke, marking the ground with our intent. With whispered vows and hands driven by energy beyond our years, we endeavored to lay to rest the specter that had haunted our nights and cast a shadow over our innocence. We whispered to the soil, weaving our hopes into its very fabric. Like prayers on the wind, our intentions carried our dreams of a world rid of the darkness embodied by the infamous warlord. We envisioned a profound hole that would swallow his malevolence, leaving the world untouched by his terror. As we dug, we etched not only into the earth but also into our very souls the power of our unity, the strength of our audacity. Like the crescendo of a symphony, our passion swelled, a chorus of innocence pushing back against the unknown. With each stroke of our fingers thrusting into the mud, we chiseled away at the fear that had threatened to engulf us. Our canvas was not just the earth; it was the annals of our shared history, a testament to the courage that blooms in the hearts of the young.

As we dug deeper into the muddy earth, a sudden sensation shivered down my spine. Something hard pressed against my fingers, triggering a primal fear within me. In my panicked state, I leaped out of the hole, convinced that a crocodile lurked beneath the surface. My frantic screams filled the air as I desperately tried to differentiate between crocodiles and alligators. This knowledge gap mattered little in the face of terror. One of my friends, calmer than the rest, reassured me that there was no immediate danger lurking beneath the mud. Reluctantly, I returned to the ground, and we continued our excavation together. With each scoop of earth, my heart pounded in my chest, my imagination running wild with images of what lay hidden beneath. And then, as if fate played a cruel trick, my hands made contact with something solid again. I yanked my hands away, my breath catching in my throat, and cried out, "It's there, it's there!" Curious and fearful, my peers jolted their hands from the mud and quickly stood up to see what I saw. As the soil parted, the truth slowly revealed itself. One of my friends remarked with surprise and grim recognition, "I know him, I know him, la ley little boy la say he was part of Ghankay army." In that sacred moment of revelation, a collective gasp rippled through the air, a sonic testimony to the profound nature of the discovery before us. Though I lacked knowledge of the boy's name or history, his visage bore the imprints of life's fragility, a canvas onto which the relentless march of time and decay had inscribed their indelible marks.

His countenance, youthful and yet etched with the scars of existence's trials, spoke volumes of life extinguished far too soon. Through the portals of his face, I beheld the chilling testimony of mortality's grasp, its fingers puncturing his once-vibrant skull, burrowing through his jaw and neck, a grim tapestry woven by the ceaseless work of earth's architects—the worms. As my gaze met his lifeless form, a cascade of emotions swelled within me—pity for the life cut short, empathy for the suffering endured, and a profound reckoning with the fragility of my own existence. In that fleeting moment of communion with the departed, we were confronted with the boy's tragic narrative and the echoes of countless lives lost to the unforgiving currents of history. I stood rooted; my gaze trapped by the haunting tableau unfurling before my young eyes. Here, death had unveiled its countenance, an encounter etched with a searing intensity that would forever brand itself upon the canvas of my consciousness. The moment's weight descended upon my tender shoulders; a mantle of emotions too immense to bear. Fear and confusion entwined with an uncanny vulnerability, each emotion vying for dominance within the chambers of my heart.

A chorus of questions, urgent and unrelenting, reverberated through the corridors of my mind. Should I hasten to the sanctuary of my mother's embrace, confiding in her the grim revelation that had unfolded? Or should I seek refuge in the shelter of a neighbor's presence, praying for their guidance in this time of turmoil? Yet, amidst this whirlwind of uncertainty, the echoes of my friend's caution resounded a sad reminder of the peril that could befall us should we unburden our secret—"If we tell anyone, we see the boy's dead body, the person that kay the boy will come to kay us too," I thought to myself. With a trembling voice, I implored my companions to conceal the gaping maw we had uncovered, an abyss that had granted us an unintended glimpse into life's fragile dance with death. And so, spurred by a shared understanding of the imminent danger that loomed, we fled the scene with all the swiftness our trembling legs could muster. Once alight with youthful exuberance, our eyes mirrored a dance of fear and vulnerability. A silent pact united us as we exchanged glances that bore the weight of our mutual distress. We draped our unease in a veil of jest and camaraderie, our laughter mingling with the remnants of dread that clung to our souls.

As the threshold of home loomed, I was enveloped by my mother's gaze, her eyes shimmering with worry and affection. "nanee, where are you coming from?" Her soothing melodic voice sought to unravel the mystery of my absence. Overwhelmed by the maelstrom of emotions that had seized my being, tears brimmed in my eyes, a reservoir of unspoken words and raw experience. In her presence, I found sanctuary—a refuge for my fractured spirit. Without needing words, she comprehended the weight of my encounter and my silence's gravity. She enfolded me in her arms, a haven of solace where understanding flowed freely, unburdened by explanations. In the embrace of her love, I discovered that words are not always necessary to bridge the chasm between hearts. In that sacred communion, the healing touch of a mother's embrace whispered of resilience, the power of shared humanity, and the unbreakable bond that transcends the unspoken depths of our lived experiences.

In the wake of those fateful days, the weight of an uninvited burden descended upon the chambers of my young heart. The image of that decaying countenance, etched indelibly into my memory, served as an unwelcome specter—a constant reminder that the veneer of our innocent pastimes concealed a darker reality where death lay in wait, poised just beneath the surface.

As time unfurled its tapestry, I found myself retreating, withdrawing into the labyrinthine corridors of my thoughts. The jovial camaraderie that once flowed effortlessly from my lips now waned, replaced by a silent solitude that echoed with the resonance of untold secrets. Like a dormant serpent, the pact of silence my friends and I had forged lay coiled within my unconscious, an unseen force that hindered the trajectory of my present progress. In those moments of introspection, I grappled with the conflicting emotions that swirled within—fear, sadness, and the weight of responsibility thrust upon my young shoulders. The burden of that silenced truth seemed to warp time, casting a shadow that extended into my interactions and endeavors. The laughter of my peers, once a symphony of shared joy, now seemed distant, as if muffled by the fog of my preoccupations.

In the wake of that harrowing revelation, the journey of Liberia pressed on, navigating the twists and turns of its tumultuous course. The scars of war, like ancient hieroglyphs etched upon the visages of survivors, spoke of a history marred by unspeakable brutality. The daily tapestry of existence, woven with threads of poverty, violence, and crumbling infrastructures, stood as a stark reminder that our beloved nation, once a beacon of promise, is now trapped within the clutches of a relentless cycle of despair. The wounds inflicted by war ran deep, carving their mark not only into the land but also into the very soul of our people. The Liberian civil war, a devastating chapter from 1989 to 2003, exacted a grievous toll, claiming the lives of more than 200,000 souls—men, women, and children whose voices were silenced by the ravages of conflict. Its aftermath bore witness to a landscape of desolation and heartache as communities lay shattered and families were cruelly sundered.

An indescribable exodus ensued, with an estimated 850,000 souls displaced, forced to flee their homes and seek refuge wherever the winds of fate might carry them. Among those displaced, many innocent children were uprooted from their families and thrust into the maelstrom of uncertainty. The echoes of those years of tribulation reverberated through time, leaving physical scars and deep-seated wounds of the heart and spirit. In the quiet spaces, amid the hushed whispers of remembrance, the true magnitude of the trauma reveals itself. The horrors witnessed, the loss endured, and the innocence robbed—all of these threads wove a tapestry of pain that extended beyond the temporal boundaries of conflict. However, the 15-year war that amassed many lives began in 1820 and totaling the deaths from 1820 to the present is a harrowing feat to reflect upon. The Liberia civil war, which reverberated worldwide, started in 1820 when White elites decided to conduct an experiment that failed. I and millions of Africans are facing the brunt of that failure. Research and studies conducted in the aftermath of the war, unveiled this collective trauma's profound and far-reaching effects on the tender canvas of children's development and well-being.

One United Nations Children's Fund (UNICEF) study revealed that an estimated 2,000 children were recruited as child soldiers during the Liberian civil war. These children were forced to witness and participate in unspeakable acts of violence, often against their communities. The psychological toll on these child soldiers was devastating, with many experiencing symptoms of post-traumatic stress disorder (PTSD), depression, anxiety, and other mental health disorders. Moreover, many children in Liberia were displaced and separated from their families during the war. According to the Internal Displacement Monitoring Centre, around 320,000 children were internally displaced within Liberia during the conflict. This displacement disrupted their education and left them vulnerable to exploitation, abuse, and neglect. Research conducted by Save the Children and the International Rescue Committee highlighted the long-term consequences of trauma on children's mental health, cognitive development, and social functioning. The prolonged exposure to violence, loss, and displacement profoundly impacted their well-being and ability to lead fulfilling lives.

Amidst the turmoil and devastation, children like myself, found themselves unwittingly thrust into the shadows of circumstance, trapped within the unrelenting grasp of violence and uncertainty. Our innocence, that precious treasure bestowed upon the young, became another casualty of the war's brutality, snatched away by the traumatic trials we were forced to endure. In the wake of this upheaval, countless children were orphaned, left adrift without the embrace of family or the shelter of a home. Their childhoods, once brimming with promise, were cast into the abyss of an unforgiving reality. The darkness of those days bore witness to a grievous sight—the forced conscription of children into the ranks of soldiers, weapons placed in their trembling hands, their fragile hearts made to bear the weight of deeds far beyond their years. The echoes of innocence lost reverberated across the battlefield, their cries a testament to the cruelty of war.

Education, a radiant beacon that once illuminated the path toward a brighter tomorrow, was shrouded in shadow during those harrowing years. Schools, once sanctuaries of knowledge, were transformed into the charred remnants of hope. Teachers, the custodians of wisdom, fled for their lives, leaving a void in their wake. The pursuit of enlightenment gave way to the grim quest for survival, and the flames of conflict consumed the dreams of a generation. The war plundered our chances for advancement, shackling us to the cycle of poverty and ignorance. Amidst this maelstrom, the pillars of healthcare groaned under the weight of chaos. Medical facilities, intended to be healing sanctuaries, were mercilessly targeted by the storm of war, leaving the wounded and ailing to fend for themselves in a world marred by strife. Disease and malnutrition, those insidious companions of conflict, took root, claiming the lives of those already teetering on the precipice of vulnerability. The welfare of the innocent young, once a sacred duty, was abandoned in the wake of chaos, their cries for help drowned out by the clamor of battle.

As I meditate on those formidable years, I come to a profound understanding: the burden of loneliness that I bore, a weight taken from the shattering of innocence, was not a solitary load I carried. Many others, my fellow Liberians, had traversed parallel trials and brought their own unique scars. It was a collective experience, a shared odyssey toward rejuvenation and reconstruction. I realized that the uncertainty, relational difficulties, parental conflicts, and constrained leadership abilities were all marred by my reluctance to confront the past. Now, the veil has been lifted, revealing that the pathway to healing from past trauma is inextricably tied to our conscious recognition of our traumas. The potency of this awareness is the crux of our recuperation journey. It serves as the fulcrum upon which we pivot toward healing. When we acknowledge the wounds we've sustained, be they as visible as cuts and bruises or as intangible as emotional scars, the pain we feel amplifies. Just as a surgeon administers anesthesia before a medical procedure, we can undergo interventions without sensing pain.

Similarly, heightened awareness serves as our psychic anesthesia. This awareness will enable us to peer into the initial stages of healing from the traumas we've experienced. However, the truth that we must bear is Liberia was experimented on, and we are the results of failed experiments; however, we are not defined by what others intended for us, but with acknowledgment of our past, we can rise above and transform our nation, people, and continent to prosper and thrive in this wicked world.

Without an awareness of our history, our future remains clouded, dimmed by the unprocessed shadows of the past. The beacon of awareness illuminates our passage toward healing. It unlocks the gateway to our restoration. However, just as we entrust medical practitioners to conduct surgical procedures, the mental health domain requires professional guiding hands. These skilled practitioners delve deep into the recesses of our struggles, facilitating the journey toward healing. Our view of the future regains clarity with the precise fusion of adept treatment and heightened awareness. At the same time, the weight of the past recedes into obscurity. The parallels between our mental and physical well-being resonate profoundly. Just as anesthesia empowers medical interventions without pain, awareness empowers our emotional healing. Awareness is the thread that weaves together every movement and change within us. Unlike knowing, which remains fixed and unchanging, awareness is dynamic, guiding us through the ebbs and flows of our journey. Our past history serves as a beacon, illuminating the path we have traversed and offering invaluable insights into our growth and evolution. With each step forward, we draw upon the wellspring of wisdom gained from our past experiences. This awareness empowers us to navigate life's twists and turns with grace and resilience, knowing that we are equipped with the knowledge needed to overcome any obstacle that may come our way.

As we embrace the profound power of awareness, we step into the realm of self-discovery and transformation. Each instance of clarity propels us forward, drawing us nearer to the essence of our true purpose. Guided by the invaluable lessons woven into the fabric of our past, we find ourselves fueled by the unwavering promise of a radiant tomorrow. In this journey, awareness transcends its mere function as a navigational tool amidst life's trials. It morphs into an infinite wellspring of inspiration and empowerment, infusing every step with purpose and vigor. Through the courageous acknowledgment of our past pain, we lay the groundwork for profound and enduring change. Yet, let us not tread this path unaccompanied. Alongside us stand mental health professionals, steadfast allies equipped with wisdom and compassion. Their presence is akin to a guiding light through the intricate labyrinth of our emotions, offering solace and guidance as we navigate the depths of our souls. In the words of Psalm 32:8, "I will instruct you and teach you in the way you should go; I will counsel you with my loving eye on you." May we find solace in the guidance of both human allies and divine wisdom as we embark on this transformative journey of self-discovery and healing.

CHAPTER 7

From Darkness To Hope

A Child's Journey Through Liberia's Civil War

My dear brothers and sisters, gather 'round as we embark on a journey through the annals of history, a journey that unravels the forgotten pages of a grand experiment, one that echoes with the hopes and dreams of a land founded on the bedrock of freedom, peace, unity, and justice for all. Liberia, a name that reverberates through time, stands as a testament to an audacious American experiment that shook the very fabric of an entire continent. Liberia, it's a name that rings with both promise and heartache. It's a name that whispers of dreams realized and dreams shattered, of a people united by a vision to forge a new destiny far from the shores they once called home. Liberia, a land bathed in both sunlight and shadow, where history's tale is a complex tapestry woven with threads of ambition, resilience, and a yearning for self-determination.

Picture the early nineteenth century, a time when the world was in turmoil, when slavery cast its dark shadow over the American landscape. Amid this tumultuous era, a group of prominent white Americans dared to dream a bold dream, a dream known as The American Colonization Society (ACS). This was no ordinary society; it was a catalyst for change, a vehicle of transformation, a conduit for the radical idea that American-born blacks could find a new home in a faraway land they knew nothing about. The ACS, in collaboration with the United States government, orchestrated a colossal endeavor, one that would forever alter the course of history. They embarked on a mission to transport black Americans and captured slaves across the vast expanse of the Atlantic Ocean to Liberia, a land of unfamiliar terrain and untold challenges. It was an endeavor of epic proportions, fueled by both idealism and pragmatism, one that tested the limits of human resilience.

In this grand experiment, we see the fingerprints of great leaders of that era, luminaries like President Thomas Jefferson and James Monroe. These were men who wielded the power to shape the destiny of nations, who saw in Liberia the possibility of Black American survivorship, an opportunity to free their brethren from the clutches of oppression and discrimination. As we delve deeper into the annals of Liberia's history, let us remember the profound courage and fortitude of those who ventured into the unknown, those who dared to carve out a new homeland, those who staked their claim to a land founded on the principles of freedom, peace, unity, and justice for all. Liberia, an experiment of monumental significance, is a story that deserves to be told, a legacy that continues to shape our understanding of resilience and determination.

In the profound words of Catherine Reef, as she penned in her book, "This Our Dark Country: The American Settlers of Liberia," we are beckoned to a chapter in history that is both poignant and complex. "Come hither, son of Africa...come; and o'er the wide and weltering sea, behold thy lost yet lovely home, that fondly waits to welcome thee." These words resonate with the resounding hope that gripped the hearts of thousands of Black Americans who embarked on a journey to Liberia, a land they believed held the promise of freedom. Indeed, this mass migration saw countless individuals crossing oceans, carrying with them not only dreams of emancipation but also the tools to build a new life and the weapons provided by the United States Government, instruments of self-defense in a world fraught with uncertainty. As they stepped onto the shores of Liberia, these pioneers were resolved to secure their newfound liberty, even if it meant demonstrating the might of American weaponry to dissuade any resistance.

In the unfolding drama of this colonization, we bear witness to a multifaceted narrative. While some indigenous Liberians extended a warm welcome to their Black American brethren, others resisted this incursion into their ancestral lands. In the face of such resistance, the settlers displayed the formidable might of American guns, a stark reminder of the immense power wielded by the newcomers. Yet, as the pages of history turn, we confront a harsh truth, one that casts a shadow over the noble aspirations of the Liberian settlers. As thousands of Black Americans settled and established themselves in Liberia, a troubling transformation occurred. In their pursuit of freedom, some among them began to emulate the very practices they had sought to escape. Tragically, there arose instances of murder, enslavement, rape, castration, and the restriction of the rights of indigenous Liberians.

This sobering reality forces us to confront the complexities of human nature and the moral ambiguities of history. The settlers, who had once yearned for liberation, found themselves grappling with the temptation to exercise dominion over others. It is a somber reminder that the quest for freedom can be a double-edged sword, one that sometimes leads to the replication of the very injustices from which one seeks escape. The story of Liberia, my brothers and sisters, is a tapestry woven with both triumph and tribulation, a tale of lofty aspirations and the stark realities of power. Liberia, born from the dreams of Black Americans seeking freedom, took its first steps towards independence in 1847, modeling its constitution, governance, policies, and laws after the United States. The very capital of this young nation, Monrovia, bore the name of American President James Monroe, a man who poured financial, physical, and intentional support into the audacious experiment of Black American survivorship in Africa.

The early years of Liberia were marked by the empowerment of Black Americans and their descendants, collectively known as Americo-Liberians. From 1847 until 1980, this minority held the reins of power, their roots tracing back to mixed-race African Americans. They established plantations and businesses, amassing wealth and, in turn, wielding overwhelming political influence. Regrettably, the governance of Americo-Liberians was marred by a deep-seated discrimination against indigenous Liberians, treating them as second-class citizens. The seeds of discontent were sown, and hardship, abuse of power, and insatiable greed pushed indigenous Liberians to their breaking point. In April 1980, a coup d'état led by Master Sergeant Samuel K. Doe of the Armed Forces of Liberia violently seized control, resulting in the tragic demise of President William Tolbert and numerous cabinet members. Samuel Doe emerged as the de facto head of state, marking the first time in Liberia's history that an indigenous leader held such a position. Doe's rule, however, was fraught with challenges.

With only a 6th-grade education, Doe governed Liberia with partiality, showing favoritism towards his tribal compatriots while ruthlessly suppressing any opposition. His actions reverberated not only within Liberia but also on the international stage, causing consternation and disapproval from the very Americans who had initiated the grand experiment. It was during this tumultuous period that former President Ellen Johnson Sirleaf, in her memoir "Madame President," shared harrowing accounts of her ordeal. She recounted how she endured molestation, imprisonment, beatings, threats, and ultimately was forced to flee her homeland due to President Doe's actions. Liberia, once a beacon of hope, had descended into chaos, crying out for strong leadership willing to make the tough decisions necessary to chart a new course.

Tragically, Doe's actions triggered a chain of events that led to the rise of another controversial figure in Liberian history, Charles G. Taylor. Taylor, who currently languishes in The Hague, faced charges of war crimes. His journey from Liberia to a U.S. jail cell, as the whispers of my childhood suggested, was indeed fraught with intrigue. The nightmare that unfolded in Liberia during those dark days, my dear brothers and sisters, is a reminder of the profound consequences of leadership, and the intricate dance of international politics. It serves as a stark testament to the complexities of history, where dreams of liberation can give way to the shadows of tyranny. As we reflect on Liberia's turbulent past, let us also pray for a brighter future, one where the lessons learned guide us towards a Liberia where justice, peace, and unity truly reign for all its people.

My dear brothers and sisters, the tale of Liberia's descent into chaos takes us deeper into the heart of darkness, where the very fabric of humanity was torn asunder. After his escape from an American jail, Charles G. Taylor embarked on a path that would forever scar our nation. He founded the National Patriotic Front of Liberia (NPFL), a rebel group driven by the fervent desire to overthrow the regime of Samuel Doe. Taylor's rebellion, ignited by grievances and fueled by vengeance, set ablaze a brutal civil war that raged on for more than a decade. The toll was staggering, as hundreds of thousands of our beloved countrymen and women perished, and millions were forced from their homes into the cruel wilderness of displacement. In the throes of this protracted conflict, Liberia became a veritable battleground, a theater of horrors where various rebel factions clashed with government forces, each side committing widespread atrocities. It was a time when the very essence of humanity seemed to wither away in the face of unrelenting violence. In this crucible of suffering, our children, the future of Liberia, bore the brunt of the tragedy.

Children, my brothers and sisters, became the most vulnerable and tragic victims of this brutal war. They were thrust into a nightmare, their innocence stolen from them by the merciless hands of conflict. Many were forcibly recruited into the ranks of child soldiers, armed with weapons, and subjected to the manipulation of the warring factions. These young souls, our sons and daughters, were thrust into a world of violence and despair that no child should ever witness. Amidst this maelstrom of chaos and cruelty, I, too, found myself entangled in the web of this nightmarish existence. As a young child, I beheld the wanton destruction of my community, the chilling specter of brutal killings that claimed the lives of family members and dear friends. The memories of those dark days continue to haunt me, a constant reminder of the cost of war and the resilience of the human spirit.

My dear brothers and sisters, the harrowing perils of war leaves an indelible mark on the human soul, a mark that can manifest in many forms. Though I have never been a soldier on the battlefield or taken another's life, I consider myself a child of war, one who has lived through and borne witness to the enduring consequences of conflict. In the crucible of war, the human mind becomes a remarkable instrument of adaptation, helping us navigate life's most unforgiving challenges. Yet, even as our minds evolve and reshape our perceptions amidst the harshest of circumstances, the haunting memories of those events persist long after the trauma has subsided.

In the year 1999, when I found myself homeless, hungry, and reduced to rummaging through refuse for sustenance, fate led me to an encounter that would forever change my perspective. It was there, in the midst of despair, that I struck up a conversation with a young man just a few years my senior. As we picked at meager scraps, he began to open up about the profound impact that the war had etched into the fabric of his life. Intrigued and empathetic, I probed further, inquiring about how this tragic chapter had left its mark upon him. For a moment, he fell silent, as if grappling with memories too painful to put into words. Undaunted by the weight of the topic, I shared a glimpse of my own journey. I explained that my parents were far away in the United States, and my homelessness was the result of being cast aside by the very person entrusted with my care, a cruel twist of fate that had forced me to fend for my own survival.

In that poignant moment of connection, the young man and I stood at the crossroads of our shared history, ready to share the burdens that war had etched into our souls. Initially, he seemed to grapple with a misunderstanding of my circumstances, but then, with a look of understanding, he posed a question that would forever alter the course of our conversation. He asked if I was prepared to hear his story, a question that carried with it the weight of a past too heavy to bear alone. Assuring him that I was ready, he proceeded to reveal a tangible reminder of his journey—a card from the United Nations. These cards, distributed by the United Nations, served as tokens of hope, encouraging young children to surrender their guns and weapons, to break free from the cycle of violence. In a somber admission, he confessed that he had once owned a weapon of destruction, a tool of war and that he had turned it in to the United Nations. Yet, despite this act of surrender, he harbored a deep-seated distrust, a profound fear of President Charles G. Taylor, a man he believed to be more wicked than any other living being. He uttered the chilling words, "Taylor is eviler than anyone alive."

Intrigued and captivated by his story, I leaned in, eager to hear the truth that lay within his heart. As he began to recount his own narrative, the world seemed to fade away, and his words filled the air like echoes from the past. He painted a vivid picture of a childhood marred by the relentless specter of war. At the tender age of five, the war had descended upon his peaceful community like a tempest. A group of rebel forces, armed with menacing AK47s, swept through the streets. What he witnessed next was a scene of unimaginable horror—a throng of hundreds, if not thousands, of people fleeing in desperation across a bridge. The chaos and fear were palpable, and in that moment, his mother, a pillar of strength, shielded his innocent eyes and urgently whisked him away from the tumultuous scene. He spoke of a father who had worked within the government, a man whose mere association with the authorities had painted a target on his back. The rebel forces possessed pictures of his father, images that signified not only his fate but also the fate of anyone connected to him—a death sentence hanging over their heads like a dark cloud.

Faced with the looming threat of persecution, he and his family were thrust into a relentless cycle of displacement, their lives forever marked by a ceaseless quest for safety. With haste, they gathered their scant belongings and embarked on a journey of perpetual movement, driven by the imperative to escape the clutches of war. Their journey was fraught with perils, as they sought refuge in the most unlikely of places—abandoned buildings, the dense cover of bushes, and the unforgiving wilderness. Their path was strewn with treacherous crossings of rivers and lakes, infested with lurking alligators and menacing crocodiles. Each step they took was laden with uncertainty, and the darkness of night offered little solace, for danger lurked in every shadow.

In this harsh existence, days would stretch into endless stretches of time, and hunger gnawed at their bellies as they scavenged for sustenance amidst the desolation. Their existence reduced to a primal struggle for survival, they consumed whatever morsels of sustenance they could find, and their lives pared down to the barest essentials. Yet, amid this cruel landscape of deprivation and desperation, tragedy struck with an unrelenting hand. His oldest sister, already weakened by the brutality of their journey, fell grievously ill. Her frail form bore the weight of suffering, and despite their desperate efforts to care for her, she succumbed to the relentless grip of sickness and was no more.

My dear brothers and sisters, the young man's story takes us to a place of profound sorrow and darkness, where the very essence of humanity seems to wither away in the face of unspeakable cruelty. As they gathered to lay his sister to rest, little did they know that the shadow of atrocity would cast its malevolent presence over their final moments together. During the solemn burial of his beloved sister, a group of militias, armed and merciless, watched as his parents, overwhelmed with grief, sought to express their final farewells. In a desperate bid to protect their son from the horrors unfolding before them, they whispered their wishes for him to hide in the concealing embrace of the nearby bushes.

The air was pierced by the deafening sound of gunfire, as the soldiers fired their weapons into the heavens, a sinister precursor to the unspeakable acts that would follow. In the cruel theater of war, three soldiers, dressed in the attire of government forces, approached the grieving parents. Their hearts devoid of compassion, they subjected the father to a savage and brutal assault, raining blows upon his head with their menacing AK47s. Tragically, his father, weakened by the relentless onslaught, fell unresponsive, his life hanging by a thread. But the horrors did not cease there, my dear brothers and sisters. The soldiers, driven by a depravity beyond comprehension, turned their malevolent attention to the defenseless mother. They violently tore away her clothes, exposing her vulnerability to their wicked desires. What followed was a nightmarish ordeal that defies the bounds of human decency, a litany of heinous acts that shatter the very soul to recount. In a voice quivering with anguish, he recounted how the soldiers callously took turns, violating every inch of his mother's body, their hands, and hearts consumed by darkness. The brutality was unimaginable, and his mother's cries must have pierced the very heavens, a desperate plea for salvation in a world devoid of humanity. In the midst of this heartbreaking tale, I became appalled and posed a question that reverberates with the pain and confusion that such stories evoke. I asked, "Where were you, Jesus? How could you watch and say or do nothing?" The silence that followed my question hung in the air like a shroud, a silence that spoke volumes of the profound grief and helplessness that enveloped that young man's soul.

He explained, he and his sister were instructed to hide in the shadows, to shield themselves from the chilling specter of the atrocities being committed. They were told to be quiet and say nothing. He explained hiding in the shadows close to his sister as they bore witness to their mother's anguished cries, her desperate shouts that pierced the night until, tragically, she too fell silent, her voice extinguished by the relentless cruelty of those who knew no mercy. Once the government forces had concluded their abhorrent actions, they marked their horrific victory with a chilling declaration. They fired their rifles into the unforgiving sky, the echoing shots serving as a chilling testament to the depths of inhumanity to which they had sunk. And then, as swiftly as they had descended upon that nightmarish scene, they departed, leaving behind a landscape forever altered by the indelible stain of their brutality.

My dear brothers and sisters, the saga of this resilient family plunges us deeper into the abyss of suffering, where the human spirit endures despite the cruelest of circumstances. After those unspeakable horrors, the father, with a heart brimming with concern, gently lifted his wounded wife, tending to her injuries with the tenderness of a loving partner. Together, they embarked on a perilous journey, navigating a landscape where danger lurked at every turn. Their path led them through the shadows of the forest, the depths of the swamp, and the unforgiving embrace of darkness. They traversed alligator-infested waters, their hearts pounding with fear, and quenched their thirst with the murky waters of the swamp. Their hunger was sated with whatever meager sustenance they could find, even if it meant eating grass. In the cloak of night, they found refuge among the dead, a haunting testament to the lengths they were willing to go to in pursuit of survival.

It was a journey that pushed the limits of human endurance, a testament to the unyielding will to live. And through the darkest of hours, they pressed on, driven by an unwavering determination to see a new day. Their odyssey eventually led them to the capital city, a place that held the promise of safety but delivered only fleeting respite. There, sleep remained a distant memory, stolen by the ceaseless alarms that shattered the night. These alarms, a chilling chorus of warning, rang out to those residing near the Executive Mansion. They served as a grim reminder of imminent danger, forcing residents to flee their homes and seek refuge on the streets. Grenades rained down upon the Executive Mansion, and the open streets became their sanctuary—a heart-wrenching choice made in the name of self-preservation. He vividly recounted the distressing routine they endured, night after night, for months on end. It was a relentless exercise, a daily ritual dictated by the cruel necessity of survival. As I listened to the young man's harrowing experiences, a deep sense of connection enveloped me, for I too had walked a path marred by the horrors of war. It wasn't merely a matter of hearing and comprehending his words; it was an empathetic bond forged in the crucible of shared suffering. Together, we bore witness to the haunting echoes of our past, seeking solace in the understanding that we were not alone in our anguish.

Just when I thought his heart-wrenching narrative had come to an end, he delved into yet another childhood story, one that bore the weight of innocence and vulnerability. He recounted a time when he was but an eight-year-old boy, filled with the boundless energy and adventurous spirit of youth. On a peaceful evening, he and his friends had gathered to partake in the universal joy of childhood—a game of soccer. During the spirited match, fate intervened with a simple kick of the ball. One of his friends sent the soccer ball rolling down a hill, a playful moment that held unforeseen consequences. In a burst of courage and determination, our young protagonist set off in pursuit of the wayward ball, his heart racing with the thrill of the chase. However, the pursuit soon led him astray, deeper into the labyrinthine landscape of uncertainty, until he found himself alone and lost.

In his desperate attempt to find his way back, he encountered a group of men in a foreboding green pickup truck. In an instant, his life took a nightmarish turn as they bound his hands, stifled his cries with a callous hand, and applied a substance to his eyes, a sinister concoction that turned them a haunting shade of red. He was transported to a camp that would forever haunt his memories, he found himself among more than a hundred children, crammed into a locked room like pawns in a cruel game. The walls of their confinement bore witness to their stolen childhoods, their laughter replaced by a palpable sense of dread. In a chilling progression of events, they were taken out of that room in groups of dozens, forced to partake in a horrifying transformation from innocent children to instruments of violence. He, too, became a part of one such group, a descent into darkness orchestrated by those who reveled in the corruption of innocence. Once in their grasp, he was handed an AK47, a weapon of death and destruction. But the targets of their training were not lifeless objects; they were fellow human beings, souls who had been captured in the merciless grip of war.

According to his harrowing testimony, they were handed AK47 rifles and subjected to a sinister trial. In this macabre ordeal, they were given three chances to hit their assigned targets. Failure to strike the target on all three attempts carried a sentence of three bullets to the head—a grotesque and nightmarish punishment. The young man found himself as the sixth person in line, trembling with fear and disbelief as he watched the gruesome spectacle unfold before him. The first boy, taller and older, took his shot and hit a girl in the chest, eliciting cheers from the rebel forces. The next boy, roughly his age, stood paralyzed, his pants stained with urine. His first shot went awry as the recoil of the gun sent it soaring uncontrollably. The second shot missed, hitting the ground, and the third struck one of the soldiers in the leg. The response from the soldiers was swift and horrifying. They seized the boy and subjected him to an unspeakable fate—shooting him multiple times in a gruesome display of violence. They went further, dismembering his lifeless body, boiling his remains, and roasting his body parts, consuming them as if they were grotesque trophies of their brutality. Shockingly, the soldier he had shot even took the boy's private parts and wore them around his neck as a sinister token. In a chilling crescendo of horror, they were forced to witness and partake in this abhorrent celebration of cruelty. The aftermath left him paralyzed with fear, unable to comprehend the depths of depravity he had just witnessed. As the nightmarish celebration concluded, another round of training began. They held their AK47 once more, and the grim cycle repeated itself. Some hit their targets, while others missed and faced the ultimate punishment—a bullet to the head. And then, my dear brothers and sisters, it was his turn. He approached the line, his heart heavy with dread, and saw a figure standing before him, a person with a red cloth covering their face, pleading for mercy. But before he could take aim, he was instructed to heed the commander's command.

In that pivotal moment, he paused, drawing upon the lessons his father had imparted about the dire importance of survival in such dire circumstances. The General, perched in a gilded chair, stared at him with an icy gaze, a bottle of alcohol in one hand and a 9mm gun in the other. His voice cut through the tension, declaring, "If I stand up, you are dead. Do not miss." With his heart pounding in his chest, he aimed, and to his astonishment, he hit the person in the head with his first shot. The commander rose from his chair, acknowledging, "That is the best shot I have seen all day." He was then directed to move to the commander's right side, where more than twenty children, who had taken the lives of people they had never seen before, stood as a grim testament to the horrors of war. They were ordered to watch as other children were commanded to kill or face death themselves.

Once they had completed these nightmarish tasks, the young man remembered that over twenty-five children, their souls forever scarred, stood alongside him, while the lifeless bodies of hundreds were dragged away. The following day, they were transported to the bush, where they encountered a witch doctor. This sinister figure created a hole in their right arms and applied a substance believed to make them invulnerable to bullets—a dark and twisted ceremony that further ensnared their souls in the clutches of evil. After this horrifying encounter, they were provided with uniforms, knives, and AK47 rifles, marking their descent into a hellish existence. The young man recounted years of moving with the rebel forces, participating in acts of unspeakable violence, including killing, rape, castration, and harm inflicted upon thousands of innocent individuals. He admitted that he was constantly under the influence of mind-altering substances, intoxicated and high most of the time, causing some actions to become hazy and indistinct in his memory. My dear brothers and sisters, as the young man concluded his haunting account, a heavy silence hung in the air, a silence that needed no words to convey the weight of the horrors he had endured. It was a moment when words seemed inadequate, and I found myself grappling with the immense pain and suffering that he had shared with such stoic resolve.

I couldn't help but wonder how he could remain seemingly unaffected by such deeply traumatic events, and my heart ached for the scars that must have etched themselves upon his soul. In an attempt to offer solace, I empathized with him and turned to the wisdom of the Scriptures, recalling Colossians 3:13, which teaches us to "Bear with each other and forgive one another if any of you has a grievance against someone. Forgive as the Lord forgave you." I shared with him the countless times that God had forgiven me and showered me with grace, even in my moments of weakness and wrongdoing. I explained that this knowledge of being forgiven had helped me choose the path of forgiveness toward others and encouraged him to seek that same forgiveness within himself.

Amid our conversation, a complex tapestry of emotions swirled within me—sadness for the unimaginable pain he had endured, empathy for his journey, and a deep desire to be an instrument of change. I reminded him that forgiveness, both of oneself and of others, is a difficult yet essential step toward healing and moving forward. It does not absolve or condone the actions committed but instead releases the burden of carrying that pain, making space for personal growth and transformation. I shared stories of individuals who had found strength in forgiveness, and who had managed to rebuild their lives despite the unimaginable circumstances they had faced. These stories were beacons of hope, proof that even in the darkest of times, the human spirit can rise above the shadows. As our conversation came to a close, I couldn't ignore the profound impact it had on me. It was an unplanned encounter, a divine appointment that had shaken the fabric of my being. Our meeting served as a stark reminder of the resilience of the human spirit, the enduring power of compassion, and the capacity for healing in the face of unimaginable darkness. His story, my story, and Liberia's painful history serve as a poignant reminder of the consequences of misguided experiments and the paramount importance of valuing human life and dignity above all else. May we, as a nation and as individuals, learn from the past and strive unwaveringly toward a future where children can grow up in a world free from violence, where their dreams are nurtured, and their potential is realized.

The pain and history of Liberia have indeed cast a dark shadow upon the lives of countless children, their innocence shattered by the greed and ego of men. But let us not forget that even in the bleakest of moments, the human spirit can shine through, resilient and unbroken. The vulnerable may suffer for a time, but with unwavering consistency, unshakable hope, and steadfast faith, they rise above their harrowing past. They emerge as survivors, bearing witness to their own stories of resilience and strength. They not only overcome their past but also conquer their future, reclaiming the promise of yesterday and shaping it into a brighter today—a today where liberty, justice, and compassion for all are not mere aspirations but lived realities. As we stand at the precipice of a new dawn, let us be guided by the lessons of our history, learning from the pain and darkness that have plagued our land. Let us pledge ourselves to a future where the nightmares of our past are replaced by the dreams of a brighter, more compassionate, and more healing.

May the stories of survival and triumph, like the one we've heard today, inspire us to work tirelessly for the well-being of our children and the prosperity of our nation. With hope as our guiding star and compassion as our compass, may we find hope, healing, and the promise of a brighter tomorrow—a tomorrow where the legacy we leave behind is one of love, unity, and justice for all. In unity and with unwavering faith, let us forge ahead on this journey toward a better Liberia, where the dreams of our children are nurtured, their potential realized, and their futures secured.

CHAPTER 8

Tachi's Waters

Navigating Loss, Guilt, and Faith - A Tribute to Moi's Memory

In the tapestry of life, some threads are woven with joy, laughter, and the warmth of friendship, while others are spun from sorrow, guilt, and the weight of loss. My childhood in Liberia was a vibrant tapestry filled with colorful threads. Still, none were as impactful as the one that wove the story of my dear friend, Moi. Moi, a towering presence of strength, courage, and boundless charisma, was not just a friend but a source of inspiration and vitality in my young life. Growing up in Liberia, a country teeming with natural beauty, rich culture, and abundant human connections, I reveled in the company of friends. Among them, Moi stood out as a beacon of resilience and vigor. Despite being three years my senior, he radiated a commanding aura that demanded respect and admiration from all who knew him. With his tall, muscular frame and a reputation for fearlessness, Moi embodied masculinity in our community. In a society where physical prowess often determined one's place, Moi's presence was an unspoken assurance of safety for those fortunate enough to call him a friend.

My earliest memories of Moi are filled with the image of him as a gentle giant. Beneath his formidable exterior lay a kind and friendly soul. He was adored by our male peers, who sought his friendship as a shield against bullies, and the girls, captivated by his tall, handsome figure. Despite his fearsome reputation, I cherished the moments we spent together, exploring the city, catching fish, playing marbles, or kicking a football with the enthusiasm only children possess. One of our cherished pastimes was visiting Moi's father's unfinished brick house. There, amidst the dusty bricks and the hum of cicadas, we would lose ourselves in games and laughter. In these moments, I felt the full extent of Moi's kindness. He treated everyone, from the smallest child to the eldest elder, with respect and friendliness. To me, that was what truly defined his character. I looked up to Moi for his physical strength and the power of his character.

Our adventures were numerous, and our shared experiences forged a bond that transcended time and space. We caught fish together, sometimes through unconventional methods like excreting in the water to attract them. Other times, we would trap them in the holes of the lake. But on that fateful day, Moi suggested something different – swimming in the Tachi River. Moi's suggestion to swim in the Tachi River was met with excitement and trepidation. We had never ventured into this particular body of water, and its depths were unknown. However, Moi's adventurous spirit was contagious, and his reassuring smile convinced us it would be an unforgettable experience. As we went to the riverbank, the sun hung high in the sky, casting shimmering reflections on the water's surface. The Tachi River flowed gently, its clear waters inviting us to plunge. The riverbanks were adorned with lush greenery, providing a picturesque setting for our impromptu adventure.

While beckoning with its tranquil beauty, the Tachi River carried unsettling legends of evil spirits that supposedly lurked beneath its surface, cunningly luring unsuspecting souls to their ominous demise. My heart wavered with hesitation, for the bitter memory of a near-drowning experience from my past still clung to my psyche. The ghosts of that encounter haunted my resolve. However, Moi's magnetic charisma and my unwavering trust in his steadfast leadership persuaded me to cast aside my trepidation and embark upon this aquatic adventure. Deep down, I firmly believed that his presence would be our safeguard, just as in countless other difficult situations we had confronted. As we ventured into the waters, the river's cool embrace sent shivers down my spine, reminding me of the eerie tales whispered by the elders around campfires. Moi's reassuring smile, however, served as a beacon of hope, casting aside the shadows of fear that had begun to creep into my thoughts. His resolute demeanor instilled in me the confidence to tread the unknown, knowing that with him by our side, we could navigate even the most enigmatic and dangerous of waters.

The sun continued its ascent in the sky, illuminating our path on the river's surface. With Moi leading the way, I found myself inching further into the river, conquering my fear of the unknown depths and my past traumas. In that transformative moment, I understood the true essence of Moi's charisma – the ability to inspire courage in the face of fear and turn apprehension into exhilaration. As we continued our aquatic journey, the tales of evil spirits faded into the background, replaced by our group's shared laughter and camaraderie. Once shrouded in ominous legends, the Tachi River became a place of unity and adventure, a testament to the power of trust and friendship that Moi had instilled in us all. Underneath the radiant sun, with Moi as our guide, we not only conquered the river but also conquered our inner demons, emerging more potent and more united than ever before. It was a day that would forever remain etched in our hearts, a testament to the transformative power of faith in the face of fear.

We frolicked in the water, our joyous laughter resonating in harmony with the gentle lapping of the river. Water fights erupted, and we competed to see who could hold their breath beneath the surface the longest. My heart, however, carried the weight of my inability to swim, casting a shadow on my playful demeanor. Beyond our shoreline playground, some other children ventured further into the river's depths. I observed them with amazement and apprehension, their graceful movements contrasting sharply with my limitations. The inability to swim was a constant reminder, and in that moment, it hung heavy on my mind.

A daring spirit gripped our companions in the deeper waters, propelling them into a spontaneous race. I watched with awe as Moi, driven by his indomitable competitive spirit, and the others playfully challenged one another to swim farther into the river. Yet, an unsettling unease began to creep over me, triggered by the tales of grown men succumbing to the river's treacherous currents and the lingering fears of evil forces that supposedly used the water as a snare for innocent souls. As the other children slowed their strokes and cautiously retreated to the safety of the shore, their voices quivering with mounting fear, Moi continued his relentless pursuit of victory. A growing sense of anxiety enveloped us all. I, too, found my voice rising in a plea for him to return. But Moi, with a mischievous grin, seemed to revel in the fear that had taken hold of his companions. His determined strokes carried him further from the shore while the others began to call out more urgently, their voices tinged with dread.

I joined their chorus, calling out to Moi in desperate tones, "Moi, Moi, Moi!" Yet, he merely paused his silhouette in the distance, turning to face us with a playful wave. At that moment, I turned around to boast about my friend's extraordinary courage and daring, but the unease and fear that had enveloped the others left me with a heavy heart. One by one, the children and adults vacated the water, their steps quickened by fear as Moi continued to swim into the unknown. As my companions scattered, their hurried footsteps echoing the whispers of superstition that gripped them, I remained steadfast, my voice resonating in the vast expanse around me. I continued to call out to my friend, Moi, my pleas carrying across the river's surface, stretching towards the distant horizon.

In my anxious vigil, I witnessed a remarkable sight. Moi, who had ventured far into the river, suddenly turned around and began swimming back towards the shore. Hope surged within me as I eagerly awaited his return. However, as I glanced at one of the children with whom he had been engaged in the race, I saw a look of sheer terror etched across the youngster's face. His round, brown eyes were stretched wide open in total shock, and his countenance bore the unmistakable imprint of fear. It was as if he had glimpsed something beyond the realm of the ordinary, something that had sent shivers down his spine. My heart quickened, and a sense of foreboding settled over me. What had transpired during Moi's daring swim? The air was tense, and the river seemed to hold its breath as if concealing a secret any of us could fathom.

Suddenly, a piercing scream cut through the air, shattering the eerie stillness that had gripped us. One of the children cried out, "He is drowning!" their voices trembling with terror. Panic spread like wildfire through the group, and in a frantic frenzy, they scattered, fleeing to their homes. I watched in utter disbelief as the older folks hastily gathered their children and departed from the river's edge, leaving a frightening scene. Amidst the chaos, I saw Moi's head briefly emerge above the water's surface, a desperate gasp for air. But as quickly as he surfaced, he vanished beneath the merciless current again. The horror of the sight was etched into my memory – the raw, unbridled fear that widened his eyes, the futile struggle against the dark abyss below. His arms flailed, his legs kicked, yet the surface eluded him. With each passing moment, precious air slipped through his desperate grasp.

He thrust his arms towards the surface in a final, valiant effort, but it was a futile struggle. The river, like an unforgiving beast, claimed him as its own. I stood there, rooted to the spot, my heart heavy with grief and burdened by an overwhelming sense of guilt. I was helpless, unable to save my friend, who had often shielded me from harm. The weight of responsibility bore down upon me, transforming into a suffocating cloak that clung to my every thought and action. Haunted by the belief that Moi's tragic demise was somehow a consequence of my fear and inability to swim, I fled from the river's edge. Seeking refuge in the solitude of my room, I was haunted by the relentless specter of guilt and grief, forever changed by the events that had unfolded by the Tachi River. My days fell into a monotonous cycle, a rigorous dance of self-doubt and isolation. I sought refuge within the four walls of my room, shutting out the world and its harsh judgments, especially from those who had known Moi and bore witness to the heart-wrenching tragedy by the river. Loneliness became my unwelcome companion, its icy grip tightening each day. The once-echoing laughter and unbreakable camaraderie of our shared adventures now felt like distant echoes, fading into oblivion. The void left by Moi's absence seemed impossible, an abyss that threatened to swallow me whole. Memories of our carefree moments haunted my waking hours, cruel reminders of what had been irreparably lost.

Weeks bled into months, and time became an elusive specter, slipping through my fingers like water, leaving me trapped in the never-ending spiral of self-recrimination. Sleep, a once comforting respite, now eluded me, replaced by restless nights filled with haunting nightmares and fragmented recollections of that fateful day. The boundary between wakefulness and dreams blurred, deepening my sense of disconnection from reality. The burden of guilt and the gaping wound of grief weighed down upon my shoulders, a relentless presence that refused to relent. I bore the heavy responsibility for my perceived failure to save Moi. Amidst the darkness that enveloped me, a longing to escape, to find redemption, clawed at the depths of my soul. Yet, the path forward remained obscured by doubt and uncertainty. How could I ever move beyond the shadow of the past when it loomed so ominously over me? The fear of judgment and the weight of blame held me captive, trapping me in a relentless cycle of self-imposed isolation, even as I yearned for a glimmer of hope and the possibility of healing.

In my darkest moments, I turned to my faith, my only anchor in a sea of uncertainty and fear. I couldn't help but tremble at the unknown path that lay ahead. The vivid dreams Moi and I had spun off his older brother's return from overseas, bearing gifts of bread, fizzy Fanta soda, and a fortune of money, now seemed like distant mirages, fading into the abyss. The dread of once again being the target of bullying, which Moi had shielded me from with his imposing presence, tightened its grip on my heart.

I sought solace in prayer, my heart pouring out its anguish in the solitude of my room. My belief in a higher power had always been a sanctuary of comfort and a wellspring of hope. I poured my thoughts and emotions into fervent prayers, praying for deliverance and mending my broken spirit. Kneeling on the cold, unforgiving floor, tears streaming down my face, I began to feel the faintest glimmer of hope. It was a fragile light amid the suffocating darkness, but it was a beginning. As I continued to pray, my mind unwittingly drifted to the cherished moments of Moi. I had shared – the laughter, the occasional conflicts, the simple meals we had savored together, and the games that had filled our days with joy. In that quiet communion with my memories, a small, tender smile began to form on my lips, even as tears continued to trickle down my face. It was a bittersweet smile, a testament to the indelible bond and the enduring friendship that had once illuminated my world.

My brother entered the room, concern etched across his face as he saw me in tears. He inquired gently, "Why are you crying?" I concocted a falsehood in my vulnerability, telling him I was overwhelmed with missing our mother. It was a white lie to shield him from the turmoil within me. He nodded understandingly and offered me a plate adorned with buttered bread and a glass filled with the comforting fizz of Fanta juice. As I devoured the simple meal hungrily, a gradual easing of the impending sense of doom began to wash over me. The shivers that had once wracked my body subsided, and I felt a glimmer of relief as though the nourishment were a balm for my soul. I reclined, yearning for the respite that sleep might bring, and tightly shut my eyes. The persistent thirst that nagged at my throat drove me to drink, and I sipped until I felt myself becoming empty once more.

The persistent urge to confide in someone weighed heavily on my heart, but the words remained elusive, slipping through my grasp like elusive shadows. How could I convey the intricate tangle of emotions that held me captive, the suffocating burden of guilt and grief? I was trapped in a labyrinth of despair, with no discernible exit in sight. The looming fear of descending into madness heightened my panic. Amidst the grief, I clung to the clothes my mother had sent me, their familiar scent offering a fragile tether to a sense of safety and love. Slowly, exhaustion overcame me, and I sank to the floor, the pain in my head momentarily subsiding. Thoughts of embracing my mother became a lifeline, tugging me away from the precipice as I drifted into a fitful slumber, desperately seeking solace in the realm of dreams.

I awakened abruptly, my heart pounding within the confines of my chest. Shrouded in a dim and unfamiliar light, it left me disoriented, struggling to discern my surroundings. As the remnants of sleep slowly dissipated, my reality's weight descended upon me again. The absence of Moi was a persistent, throbbing ache in the depths of my soul. This ever-present specter served as a haunting reminder of the heart-wrenching tragedy that had unfolded at the Tachi River. Each passing day since that fateful event had become an arduous battle against the relentless forces of guilt and grief. Yet, the loss of my dear friend, Moi, and the subsequent emotional turmoil I grappled with are not isolated incidents. Drowning accidents, like the one that claimed Moi's life, tragically occur all too frequently, leading to the untimely loss of countless lives on a global scale. Among the victims, a significant portion comprises young souls whose futures are abruptly extinguished. These stark statistics serve as a sad testament to the critical importance of water safety measures and the urgent need for comprehensive prevention strategies to safeguard the lives of our loved ones.

The gravity of such incidents transcends mere statistics; they reach into the hearts and minds of our children, leaving an indelible mark on their tender souls. Children who witness the loss of a dear friend are thrust into a tumultuous sea of emotions, navigating a complex range of feelings that can have far-reaching consequences. In 2023, the data regarding water-related tragedies is undeniably distressing, particularly when we consider its profound impact on our future's young and impressionable minds. Among the haunting effects, we find the specter of survivor's guilt, a weighty burden that children often shoulder. They grapple with a profound responsibility for the incident, even when it is beyond their control. This self-imposed blame becomes a heavy yoke that stifles their youthful spirit and casts shadows over their lives. The emotional turmoil they experience can hinder their ability to cope and move forward, casting a pall over their mental well-being and overall development.

The data from 2023 underscores the critical need for us, as a society, to address not only the tangible aspects of water safety but also the intangible, yet equally significant, emotional repercussions. As we strive to implement preventive measures and foster a water safety culture, we must also extend our collective embrace to those young hearts burdened by grief and guilt. In our mission to safeguard lives, we must also become guardians of the emotional well-being of our children. Through providing them with the support, understanding, and resources they need to navigate the complex terrain of their emotions. Through this holistic approach, we can ensure that the ripples of a tragic incident do not become impossible waves that threaten to drown the hopes and dreams of our youth.

It is imperative to recognize the profound psychological impact that traumatic events can have on children who bear witness to them. As parents, caregivers, and communities, it has become our sacred duty to establish sanctuaries of safety where these young souls can courageously and openly articulate their emotions. Equally vital is the readiness to seek professional assistance when the need arises, for it is a crucial step in their healing journey. By extending a hand of understanding, unwavering compassion, and sage guidance, we can play a pivotal role in guiding these precious young souls through the turbulent aftermath of such harrowing experiences. Reflecting on my own life, I must acknowledge that I was not privileged to receive the support I desperately needed to confront the trauma that enveloped me when I witnessed my dear friend's drowning. It wasn't until I reached adulthood and made numerous regrettable missteps that I finally grasped trauma's insidious hold on my existence. Faith provides hope in these profound moments of loss and grief. As I knelt in my room, pouring my heart into fervent prayers, I began to grasp the transformative power of faith in the healing process. Through faith, I discovered the strength to confront my overwhelming guilt and sorrow, embarking on a journey of forgiveness towards myself and Moi. My belief in my capacity for resilience propelled me from the depths of darkness into a realm of boundless possibilities.

The undeniable truth is that healing from the searing wounds of loss is a gradual journey that demands time, self-compassion, and the unwavering support of cherished loved ones. Yet, it is crucial to underscore that without faith in oneself, the required profound internal healing may remain elusive. Through faith, coupled with the deep realization that certain burdens are not meant to be borne in isolation, I began stitching together the tattered fabric of my soul. Moi's memory remains etched in the recesses of my heart, a poignant reminder of life's fragility and the extraordinary resilience of the human spirit, capable of enduring and ultimately healing. As I continue my recovery path, I aspire to become a beacon of hope for those who have weathered similar storms of tragedy. Together, fortified by faith, deep understanding, and the unifying strength of community, we can navigate the tumultuous waters of grief and eventually arrive at the shores of healing and resilience. The narrative of Moi and the profound impact of his loss on my life serves as a testament to the enduring human capacity for forgiveness, growth, and transformation. It is a story of redemption, which I earnestly hope will kindle the flames of inspiration in others, guiding them toward their unique paths to recovery and inner peace.

CHAPTER 9

Bluebird

A Tale Of Unbreakable Friendship And Healing

Have you ever been blessed with that one extraordinary friend, a true confidant destined to stand by your side unwaveringly, regardless of life's challenges? That cherished companion who possesses the remarkable ability to delve into the depths of your thoughts, to lend an ear to your words, and to effortlessly coax a smile upon your countenance even in your moments of deepest despair. Picture the kind of friend whose affectionate embrace of your soul is so profound that each morning's awakening is accompanied by the unwavering certainty of their boundless love, reciprocated wholeheartedly by your own. The beacon of my dearest friendship was ignited at the tender age of five when my best friend graced my life with her presence. Her eyes, a mesmerizing shade of brown, sparkled like precious gems, reflecting the depth of her spirit. Cascading waves of golden hair framed her countenance, framing a visage that bore witness to an extraordinary nature and a captivatingly flirtatious and engaging demeanor. Fear was a foreign concept to her, and she effortlessly commanded attention in every corner she ventured into, an inexhaustible reservoir of vivacity.

She radiated an utterly infectious exuberance, a ceaseless whirlwind of vitality that left an indelible mark wherever her footsteps danced. She existed in a perpetual state of readiness, forever eager to embark on whimsical escapades and daring exploits, her zest for life inspiring even the most reticent souls to join in the jubilation. Whether we found ourselves frolicking in the midst of playful adventures or seeking solace beneath the sheltering canopy of the plum tree, she was my steadfast companion, an attentive listener to the tales of my heartache and tribulations. In her presence, trust blossomed like the most delicate of flowers, unfurling its petals in the radiant sunlight of our unbreakable bond. Amidst the backdrop of a country where the assurance of tomorrow was far from a guarantee, I found myself imprisoned by a paralyzing fear, a fear that erected walls around my heart, preventing me from extending my trust or affections to another. But in the midst of this emotional fortress, a divine exception emerged, and that exception was none other than my cherished confidante, Bluebird. She materialized as a beacon of light, the sole being upon whom my heart bestowed instant love and unwavering trust.

In a realm where the act of tomorrow's arrival was an elusive promise, we, the youthful culprits, orchestrated escapades that danced on the edges of audacity, like purloining the succulent treasures of mangoes from the encroaching grasp of our neighbor's yard. It was in the intoxicating innocence of these exploits that I tasted the sweetness of my first kiss, a stolen moment exchanged amidst the spirited game of "Hide and Seek." Yet, even as we savored these stolen tastes of delight, life itself cast its ominous shadow. Together, we bore witness to the heart-wrenching tragedy of a beloved friend's untimely demise by drowning. The weight of grief pressed upon our tender souls, forging an unbreakable bond through shared sorrow. And when the tumultuous tides of change ushered my parents to distant shores, seeking a brighter tomorrow in the embrace of the United States, Bluebird was the constant amidst the upheaval.

She remained my steadfast companion through skirmishes and battles, a sentinel of loyalty during nights spent seeking refuge within forsaken dwellings and the cavernous shelter of cars. Even during the direst of moments, when the scavenging for sustenance within refuse bins became a stark reality, Bluebird stood by my side, unwavering in her devotion. In the symphony of chaos that life composed, she emerged as the tranquil note, the unyielding foundation upon which I could build my resilience. My rock, unyielding in its support. My foundation, unwavering amidst the shifting sands of existence. My peace, a sanctuary of solace amid the cacophony of trials and tribulations. During the tempests of trauma that assail us, we often find ourselves standing solitary, engaged in battles that stretch the limits of our strength. We grapple with the abyss of emotional turmoil, navigate the labyrinthine corridors of our minds, and even endure the weariness that infiltrates our very physical being. In these moments of overwhelming adversity, we're left yearning for an anchor, a presence to help us decipher the cryptic language of the challenges that confront us.

Yet, there was a luminary in my life, a celestial being who defied the odds and remained steadfast by my side. Bluebird, the embodiment of steadfastness and unwavering companionship, emerged as my guiding light. Amid life's tempestuous storms, she stood tall as a beacon of unwavering support, a constant reminder that I was not alone in this arduous journey. With her unwavering presence, she etched an indelible mark upon the tapestry of my existence. She was not merely a friend; she was the very essence of empathy, compassion, and strength. As the tempests raged and the tides of adversity threatened to consume me, Bluebird was the tranquil harbor where I could find solace. Her unwavering companionship was the lifeboat that kept me afloat, rescuing me from the drowning depths of isolation.

The struggles we encountered were no longer solitary battles fought in the shadows. With Bluebird by my side, the battles transformed into shared endeavors, a testament to the unbreakable bond that tethered us together. She infused my life with courage, whispered hope in times of despair, and illuminated the darkest corners of my soul with her unwavering presence. In an era where loneliness often emerges as an unwelcome companion during trials, she defied the odds, standing tall as a testament to the power of genuine friendship. With Bluebird as my stalwart ally, I was fortified against the fiercest of life's tempests. She embodied the spirit of togetherness, teaching me that even amidst the storm, we can find solace in the presence of a true friend.

Indeed, every passing day, the ache within my heart resonates with a poignant melody of absence. I am acutely aware of her absence, a vacancy that no passing time can ever fill. Her nature, marked by an insatiable curiosity that mirrored the wonder of a child's first steps into the world, and an aura of protective energy that enveloped me like a guardian angel, is a symphony I yearn to hear once more. The sweet memory of her affectionate kisses and tender hugs becomes a bittersweet refrain that echoes within the chambers of my soul. The memory of our shared walks and exhilarating runs, where the world blurred around us, leaving only the pulse of our synchronized steps, fills my heart with a wistful longing. How I pine for the reassuring touch of her paw against my hand, a gesture that transcended words and spoke of an unspoken bond. Her gaze, a mosaic of understanding and empathy, was a balm for my sadness, a gentle reminder that in the shadows of despair, I was not alone. During times of confusion, her presence was an unwavering compass, pointing me toward clarity with each thoughtful glance.

The yearning within me extends beyond mere physical companionship; it reaches for the very essence of her being. I crave the warmth of her trust, a trust unmarred by doubt or hesitation, a bond that held us together like an unbreakable thread woven by destiny. Her protection, like an impenetrable shield, enveloped me, creating a sanctuary in which my vulnerabilities were safe to emerge. Her intelligence was a marvel, a reminder that wisdom often wears the guise of a four-legged friend. The pride she carried, not in arrogance, but in a regal elegance that proclaimed her rightful place in the tapestry of existence, was a sight to behold. Everywhere we journeyed, she walked with a grace that bespoke her inherent nobility, leaving an indelible impression upon all who crossed her path. And then, that fateful day, when the news of her departure fell upon my ears like a lament, my world was suspended in a paradox. My stomach, nourished, yet empty—full of sustenance, yet devoid of comfort. My mind, heavy with the weight of unbearable grief, a pain that defies articulation. The pain, an intangible agony that transcends the realm of the physical, serves as a testament to the depth of our connection, a bond that not even death can sever. In the absence of her physical presence, the pain becomes a haunting reminder of the many memories we shared, especially the last moment I saw her aches through my soul, a day I will never forget.

In the annals of February 1999, a chapter of my history was penned alongside my dear companion, Bluebird. On that cherished day, we embarked upon a journey to the river's edge, driven by the dual purpose of partaking in its refreshing waters and securing sustenance to appease our hunger. With hopeful hearts, we embarked upon this venture, driven by the innate survival instincts that often emerge during times of adversity. Our efforts proved fruitful, as the river yielded an abundant harvest of fish, glistening in the sunlight as if offering themselves willingly to our need. With jubilation coursing through our veins, we ventured into the embrace of the verdant grasses that lined the riverbank. There, among nature's bounty, we foraged for wood, each piece a potential key to unlocking the nourishment we so desperately craved. With resourcefulness as our guide, we harnessed the primal element of fire. Using the nearest rock as a testament to the ingenuity of our spirits, we sparked flames that danced with newfound vitality. The crackling warmth of the fire became a hearth upon which our hopes were roasted alongside the fish, turning sustenance into a shared communion of provision and fellowship. With every sizzle and aroma that graced the air, our bond grew stronger, entwining our souls through the simplest yet most profound act of breaking bread, or in this case, sharing the fruit of the river.

The river's edge, which had borne witness to our endeavors, now embraced our gratified forms. Our bellies, once echoing hollowly with hunger, were now content and full. Yet, the looming specter of homelessness cast its shadow over us, a reminder that even amid moments of satiation, our journey was a rugged one, defined by the challenges of uncertainty. As the sun gracefully descended beneath the horizon, imbuing the canvas of the sky with the gentle brushstrokes of dusk, our hearts sought solace within the embrace of an abandoned edifice. This silent sentinel, a relic of forgotten days, whispered the tales of those who had tread its halls before us. The echoes of bygone lives reverberated through its weathered walls; an ethereal reminder of the human stories interwoven with the fabric of time.

Within these timeworn confines, we fashioned a sanctuary born from the crucible of our collective resilience, a haven sculpted from the very essence of our spirits. This dilapidated structure, witness to the ebb and flow of countless lives, became a testament to the tenacity that arises when faced with the crucible of adversity. We, two souls bound by circumstance and friendship, erected a bastion of hope within these aged walls, turning destitution into a canvas upon which our strength was painted. Amid the shroud of night, as the stars above us twinkled like guardian sentinels, our souls found sanctuary within the arms of this forsaken refuge. Here, in this forgotten alcove, we surrendered to the symphony of nature's lullabies. The hoots of owls, the chorus of frogs, and even the gentle cadence of our own breathing became the soundtrack of our respite. As our bodies reclined, sated by the fruits of our labor, we surrendered ourselves to the embrace of slumber, a profound rest that was earned through the toil of the day.

As we nestled into the folds of the night, it was not merely our bodies that sought rest; our very souls sought restoration within the quietude of the darkness. It was within this sanctuary of reclaimed solitude that our hearts found respite, our minds found tranquility, and our beings found unity with the rhythms of existence. Our slumber, punctuated by the soft symphony of owls' hoots and the gentle rustling of the night, was a testament to the harmony that can be found even within the most desolate of circumstances. Thus, within the hallowed space of that forsaken structure, as the night enfolded us in its tender embrace, we surrendered to the rhythm of the universe. We closed our eyes, our bellies full and our spirits renewed, allowing the tapestry of dreams to carry us away, guided by the whispered secrets of the stars and the gentle touch of time With the dawning of the next morning, the first rays of light cast their hopeful glow upon my awakening, only to reveal the absence of a vital presence that had been woven into the very fabric of my existence. As the realization swept over me like a gust of wind, a frantic urgency gripped my heart, propelling me into a relentless pursuit that would unravel the depths of my determination. In a frenzy fueled by equal parts fear and longing, I embarked on a quest that knew no boundaries. Every corner of our community bore the weight of my relentless search, as I implored each soul I encountered about the whereabouts of my beloved Bluebird. In some instances, my inquiry was met with the sting of laughter, an echoing mockery that only served to ignite the fires of my determination. In others, averted gazes and clenched jaws spoke volumes, painting a picture of silent knowledge shrouded in secrecy.

The rivers, once tranquil and familiar, were now transformed into arenas of hope and trepidation. With every ripple that caressed the riverbanks, I strained my eyes, seeking a glimpse of the one who had etched an indelible mark upon my heart. The bushes whispered secrets to the wind, and the markets pulsed with the rhythm of life, yet my quest remained unfulfilled. I ventured into the depths of every dwelling, knocking on doors that held the promise of reunion, only to be met with the hollow echoes of disappointment. The sun climbed higher in the sky, casting its warm glow upon my determined journey. With each step, a plea reverberated within my being, a plea to the universe to guide me to the missing half of my soul. The shadows grew longer as the day progressed, and the weight of uncertainty settled upon my shoulders like an invisible burden.

In the midst of this desperate odyssey, I realized that the search for Bluebird had transcended the physical realm; it had become an embodiment of the profound connection we shared. Our bond, once so tangible, had now become an ethereal thread that traversed the landscape of memory and longing. With each unanswered question and each door left unopened, the journey itself morphed into a testament to love's unwavering persistence. As the sun began its descent once again, painting the sky with the hues of twilight, I stood at the crossroads of determination and surrender. My quest had unearthed not just the depths of my longing, but also the vastness of the community's secrets. And though the physical form of Bluebird eluded me, her spirit lingered in every corner, a reminder that true companionship transcends the boundaries of time and space. In the wake of the day's arduous journey, I found myself enveloped by the enigmatic embrace of the night. With a heart heavy with unanswered questions, I retreated from the realm of the community, finding solace beneath the veil of stars. The echoes of my search, the hushed whispers of the unyielding quest, became intertwined with the symphony of crickets and rustling leaves. And as I closed my eyes, the void left by Bluebird's absence was filled with the symphony of memories and the reverberation of a bond that would forever echo within the chambers of my heart.

As the relentless march of days pressed onward, my quest remained unyielding. My unwavering determination clashed with the growing weariness of those around me, their patience frayed by my ceaseless inquiries regarding the whereabouts of Bluebird—a companion deemed insignificant by their limited vision. The refuge I once found within abandoned cars now appeared as a faded memory, and the once-familiar streets of the neighborhood had transformed into a labyrinth of uncertainty without the reassuring presence of my faithful friend by my side. Yet, against the backdrop of doubt, I held onto the flicker of hope that illuminated my path.

The path of my search led me to an unexpected crossroads, a junction where my determination brushed against the edge of trepidation. It was here that I found myself standing before a neighbor, a figure whose reputation was tinged with shadows of darkness. Whispers of his actions reverberated through the community—an ominous aura of someone who had been rumored to have committed unthinkable acts. With a heart heavy with both fear and hope, I mustered the courage to look into his eyes and articulate my inquiry about Bluebird. To my astonishment, sincerity resonated within his voice as he reassured me, promising that he would never bring harm to my beloved companion. This unexpected exchange, marked by an offering of nourishment, transformed my perception. A generous bowl of fufu and soup, laden with succulent morsels of meat, alleviated the gnawing pangs of hunger that had plagued me. I consumed the sustenance with a fervor born from the understanding that this meal, so graciously provided, was a testament to the unexpected threads of kindness that can weave through the tapestry of even the most challenging circumstances.

In that fleeting moment, as I partook in the sustenance he offered, gratitude unfurled within me like a blossoming flower. The sheltering arms of safety and love, though ephemeral, enveloped me in their embrace. Amidst the absence of my parents, this seemingly ordinary gesture became a beacon of light, a reminder that even in the bleakest moments, human connection can emerge as a lifeline.

Yet, destiny, with its enigmatic twists, had more to unveil. A week later, a peer who had once scorned my pain emerged from the shadows of his past indifference. Compassion guided him toward my tear-stained presence, the weight of empathy evident in his gaze. In words that struck me like a thunderclap, he revealed the unthinkable truth—that a neighbor we knew well had extinguished the radiant light that was Bluebird. The very air I breathed felt poisoned by this revelation as if I had been plunged into a nightmarish realm from which there was no escape. I unleashed a torrent of grief, a symphony of tears, cries, and desperate pleas that reverberated through the air.

Tears flowed unabated down my cheeks, leaving a trail of salt water as testament to the anguish that overwhelmed me. In a daze, I retraced my steps, the journey back to the abandoned car, a slow march of sorrow. Each footfall felt like a burden too heavy to bear, the truth settling in the pit of my stomach like a leaden weight. The nausea that clawed at me found release in an uncontrollable bout of vomiting, a visceral response to the unimaginable reality that had been thrust upon me. I cried, my tears mingling with the remnants of my torment.

The revelation that I had consumed the flesh of my cherished companion unknowingly became an abyss that threatened to swallow my very essence. The emptiness that gnawed at my core was matched only by the whirlwind of thoughts that swirled in my mind, thoughts that danced along the edges of self-inflicted pain. A desolate resolve gripped me as I ventured toward the river's depths, my heart heavy with a burden too great to carry. The waters beckoned, an enigmatic embrace that held the allure of release from the unbearable weight I bore. Yet, fate, in its unerring wisdom, intervened once more. The watchful eyes of strangers, mere passersby who noticed my intent, became the lifelines I had unknowingly sought. They pulled me from the depths of despair, their words carrying a potent warning that echoed with the weight of concern. The threat of revealing my intentions to my older brothers held within it a testament to the interconnectedness of human compassion, a reminder that even in the darkest hours, a lifeline can materialize from the unlikeliest of sources.

The echoes of that near-tragic moment lingered as I navigated the caverns of grief that lay before me. In the silence of my solitude, a profound void loomed, a void where Bluebird once walked beside me, an inseparable presence. In the realm of sustenance, our unity was defined by the rhythm of shared meals. Her comforting touch had once offered solace to my tears, and her presence provided warmth against the cold embrace of the night. In my moments of vulnerability, Bluebird had been the steadfast foundation upon which I leaned, the unwavering pillar that absorbed the weight of my sorrow. I became burdened with a sense of complicity in her demise, a feeling akin to a guilt-ridden accomplice who had unknowingly betrayed a dear friend. With each utterance of my pain, the act of sharing my wounds with my peers became a cathartic release. In their stories of Bluebird's strength, her resilience became a mirror reflecting my own spirit. Their voices, like soothing salve, offered a measure of solace that began to temper the intensity of my anguish. Though the weight of her loss remained heavy, I was comforted by the realization that her memory endured through the stories we shared.

Yet, the specter of her tragic end remained an unshakeable presence within my psyche. It was a burden that could have consumed me, chaining me to the past with unbreakable bonds. But in the midst of my pain, I gleaned a profound truth—the past, no matter how agonizing, need not dictate the trajectory of our future. It is within our power to choose how our experiences shape us, to transform pain into purpose, and to weave the threads of healing into the tapestry of our lives.

The journey of genuine healing is a profound odyssey that necessitates delving into the recesses of our own souls, confronting the shadows that dwell within, and mustering the courage to unmask our vulnerabilities. It's a testament to our shared humanity—an intricate dance of authenticity and vulnerability that inspires others to embark on their own transformative journeys. However, societal expectations and cultural norms often shroud our true selves in silence, causing us to stifle our authenticity. In truth, the process of healing is a communal tapestry, woven from the threads of shared experiences—identities such as race, gender, religion, and culture intertwining to create a mosaic of understanding. In particular, for individuals of color who find themselves in foreign lands, the quest for healing is compounded by the challenges of assimilation and the quest for belonging. The journey commences within, where we conduct a painstaking internal audit, unearthing the traumas that have shaped us and the steps necessary to heal. Through vulnerability, we attain a profound self-awareness—a recognition of our own interconnectedness with human experience. This awakening unveils the intricate web of trauma, sorrow, and joy that has woven the fabric of our lives. By embracing this complex tapestry, we find solace in the acknowledgment of our past, gaining the strength to hold our experiences with grace.

Yet, the very act of vulnerability, this revealing of our most authentic selves, often leaves us vulnerable to the gnawing fear of judgment. A perception of weakness, should we allow our vulnerability to be seen, shadows this path. And yet, the journey toward healing beckons us to cast aside these fears, inviting us to courageously unveil our truths. From the depths of despair emerged a profound lesson—a lesson in cherishing the bonds that form the tapestry of our lives. The loss of Bluebird illuminated the sanctity of friendship, the power of love, and the depths of compassion. Through her absence, I learned to reach out to others, expressing gratitude for their presence and support. Empathy took root within me, a profound understanding that each person carries their burdens, their stories, their hidden scars. In truth, acknowledging trauma, I learned, is not a submission to its grasp; rather, it is a pivotal step on the path of healing. Through the intricate dance of acceptance and resilience, I began to navigate the labyrinthine corridors of recovery. The scars left behind by the trials I faced may forever be a part of my story, but they no longer define the entirety of who I am. Instead, they serve as reminders of my capacity for survival, my strength in the face of adversity, and my ability to forge a path forward despite the weight of the past.

In the wake of Bluebird's departure, the ache of loss gradually metamorphosed into a poignant testament to the love that once flourished between us. Her absence, once a void, now serves as a gentle reminder of the profound connections we forge in this fleeting existence. Within me, her spirit dwells as a comforting presence, a guiding light that illuminates the path of nurturing and cherishing those we hold dear. The legacy of Bluebird transcends the confines of time, weaving itself into the very tapestry of my being. Through her, I have come to understand the enduring qualities of loyalty, resilience, and the transformative power of love. In her memory, I have discovered a wellspring of healing and fortitude, transforming my grief into a beacon of solace and hope for others on their own journeys of healing.

In the words of Elisabeth Kübler-Ross, 'The reality is that you will grieve forever. You will not 'get over' the loss of a loved one; you will learn to live with it. You will heal and you will rebuild yourself around the loss you have suffered. You will be whole again, but you will never be the same. Nor should you be the same nor would you want to.'" Guided by Bluebird's eternal presence, I navigate life's trials with a newfound resilience, knowing that her love and friendship remain steadfast, ever watchful from the celestial heights above. Thus, in the intricate tapestry of existence, her legacy endures—a testament to the profound lessons of companionship, resilience, and the enduring power of love.

CHAPTER 10

Breaking The Chains

Transforming Leadership Through Healing And Resilience

In the ever-evolving landscape of entrepreneurship and the relentless pursuit of progress and success, it is paramount to recognize that the true cornerstone of any flourishing endeavor lies in the well-being of those who drive it forward. Just as a garden thrives when tended to with care, so do the minds behind every innovative idea, strategic move, and game-changing decision that shapes our world. Amidst the ceaseless hustle and the never-ending to-do lists that define our professional lives, the silent battles we wage within ourselves can often be relegated to the background. Nevertheless, an undeniable truth remains: a healthy mind serves as the catalyst for creativity, resilience, and sustainable growth.

The journey towards prosperity is not a mere sprint; it is a marathon of challenges and opportunities. Similar to how bodybuilders sculpt their physical strength, leaders must diligently cultivate their mental resilience. In carving out space for self-care, mindfulness, and open conversations about mental health, where we unleash a ripple effect that reverberates throughout ourselves and the ones we lead. Taking care of ourselves as leaders sets a powerful example for our teams. When we prioritize our well-being, we inspire our colleagues to do the same. This creates an environment where stress turns into problem-solving, burnout transforms into renewed passion, and teamwork flourishes through empathy and understanding.

By embedding self-care principles into our leadership approach, we cultivate a culture where mental health isn't just a box to tick off but a continuous commitment. This ensures that our teams thrive and that we all work together in a supportive and productive way. In this collective effort to nurture our mental well-being, we elevate not only ourselves but also those we lead, inspiring them to perform at their best. However, there is Leadership, I firmly believe, extends beyond the confines of our professional lives. In fact, each one of us possesses the capacity for leadership in our own unique way. What often obstructs our path to leading our lives to the fullest potential is the internal battle we wage against ourselves. Our inability to confront the truths within us often keeps us in denial, perpetuating a cycle where we continue to dwell in the shadows of our childhood pain. This unresolved pain can severely limit our ability to excel and reach the highest echelons of our lives. In the wisdom of Bishop TD Jakes, we find guidance on the path to self-realization and effective leadership. He reminds us that confronting our inner demons and facing the unvarnished truth about ourselves are pivotal steps toward personal growth and empowerment. Only when we shed light on the darkness within can we begin to heal and rise above our past traumas.

In essence, true leadership begins with leading ourselves towards a healthier, more resilient mental state. It is a journey of self-discovery and self-care that paves the way for us to lead others with empathy, compassion, and authenticity. By recognizing the significance of mental well-being and taking proactive steps to nurture it, we not only enhance our own lives but also create a ripple effect of positive change in our organizations and communities. From the earliest moments etched in my memory, I have held within me a burning aspiration: to mirror the resolute spirit of my father, a man whose essence is characterized by a quiet yet unyielding determination, and an unwavering commitment to chasing after his dreams. His life has breathed inspiration into my veins, urging me to reach for the stars with the same vigor that courses through his veins. His existence, a tapestry woven with threads of scholarship, servitude, and fatherhood, has fashioned an intricate map for me to navigate the world.

Yet, the brilliance of my father's leadership extends far beyond the borders of his individual qualities. The chapters of his life read like the epic tale of a guardian during Liberia's tempestuous times. He stood steadfast as a security officer, safeguarding President Samuel Doe, even as the storm clouds of political turmoil gathered ominously. Those were days when the fabric of our lives was woven with threads of danger, and the air was heavy with the scent of uncertainty. President Doe's tragic end at the hands of warlord-turned-president Charles Taylor thrust us into a perilous spotlight. Those associated with President Doe bore a bullseye, a target painted upon their very souls. Yet, in the face of such peril, my father emerged as a beacon of courage, a true hero. Through his valor, our family persevered. But his heroism was not confined to presidential corridors. Beneath his official role, my father's heartbeat in rhythm with a commitment to education. He stood side by side with his mother, helping her raise five public schools from the dust of aspiration to the pillars of reality. Even during the ceasefire amidst the cacophony of war, he flung open the doors of education, an oasis of hope amidst the desert of turmoil. Leaders, present and former, were drawn to the light he kindled. Witnessing his dedication to the noble cause of learning has left an indelible mark on my soul.

In a world woven with intricate challenges, where uncertainty lurks at every turn, the beacon of my father's example is a reassuring lighthouse. His life narrative reveals the potency of resilience, the art of selfless service, and the essence of authentic leadership. It's a legacy that has become a part of my DNA, a compass guiding my path forward. In honor of his tireless journey, in reverence of his unwavering commitment, I stand resolute. I am resolute in my determination to spread positive ripples across the lives of others, just as he has done for our family and the countless others who have been touched by his light in Liberia.

Leadership, my friends, is a journey of both light and shadow, a profound odyssey that unveils its challenges and triumphs, its burdens and blessings. It is a sacred call that beckons us to step onto a path where unhealed wounds and enduring pain can cast a shadow over the very essence of our leadership. You see, the tapestry of leadership is woven from the threads of our life experiences, the strands of our past that shape our present and color our decision-making. I've known this truth intimately, for I too have walked the path strewn with the thorns of solitude. It was in the depths of that isolation, in the midst of the darkest times, that I unearthed a gift— a gift that whispered of my capacity to be a beacon of change amidst the shadows. Gazing at the blueprint set forth by my father, a man of unwavering determination and relentless pursuit of his dreams, I aspired to lead in the same noble manner. The pillars of leadership, etched in sacrifice, commitment, and unwavering service, stood tall before me, beckoning me forward.

Yet, dear souls, there lies a profound paradox within leadership—one that mandates that we tread carefully, for leading while carrying the weight of unhealed trauma can inadvertently sow seeds of pain, not only within ourselves but also in the lives we yearn to serve. Our past, dear friends, possesses the power to shape us, to influence our intentions and decisions. And though we strive to cast our leadership in the light of nobility, the shadows of our unaddressed wounds can cast a pall over our journey. A memory from my own young years emerges—an incident etched into the annals of my existence when, at the tender age of eleven, I found myself thrust into a leadership role, my parents absent in a time of dire need. What I witnessed then, my dear companions, is a scene that indelibly marked my consciousness—a young man, besieged by a relentless onslaught from a throng of over twenty. The anguished cries of mothers reverberated through the air, their voices carrying the weight of violated innocence, and the plaintive wails of little girls echoed their grief, their tears mirroring the void left by a father's untimely demise.

There, in the crucible of that moment, I stood as a silent sentinel, witnessing a spectacle that defied the bounds of compassion. The air was thick with the scent of aggression, as fists and feet met flesh with ruthless fury. Kicks, punches, slaps—violence unabated, as rocks were hurled like missiles. But amidst that symphony of brutality, a spark ignited within me—the spark of courage, of empathy, of a determination to rise above the tumult and intervene. The path to leadership, my dear friends, is paved with risks, with moments that dare us to stand firm against the tempest of injustice. And so, with every ounce of my young courage, I stepped into the maelstrom, a beacon of hope amidst a sea of chaos. It was in that defining moment that my leadership found its true purpose. As chaos began to erupt a police officer eventually materialized, a figure of authority whose intervention, like a soothing balm, quelled the storm of hatred that raged around us. The fates of those involved remained shrouded in mystery, their stories absorbed into the ever-shifting sands of time. My bravery and foolery to be honest was done without thought but I recalled acting and through my action a life was safe.

My dear brothers and sisters, I stand before you today as a humble witness to the transformative power of healing, resilience, and the unyielding spirit of leadership. In the tapestry of life, we are often woven with threads of unhealed wounds and untold pain, threads that can cast shadows over the very leadership we aspire to embody. Yet, let us not forget that within the confines of these shadows lies the potential for profound growth, for the emergence of leaders who rise above adversity, inspire change, and illuminate the path to a brighter future. Leadership, my friends, is a sacred calling—a calling that beckons us to step into the role of change-makers, influencers, and guides. It is a calling that demands our unwavering commitment, our relentless pursuit of excellence, and our willingness to stand in the face of adversity with unyielding courage. Yet, within this pursuit of greatness, we sometimes overlook the importance of tending to our own wounds, confronting the traumas that have shaped us, and acknowledging the shadows that cast their pall over our journey.

I, too, have walked this path, a path fraught with challenges, triumphs, and the unrelenting specter of unaddressed trauma. As I reflect upon my journey, I am reminded of the words of renowned leaders who have grappled with their own failures and scars. Their experiences resonate deeply, shedding light on the profound impact that unhealed trauma can have on leadership. Albert Einstein, a brilliant mind who reshaped our understanding of the universe, once said, "The world will not be destroyed by those who do evil, but by those who watch them without doing anything." These words remind us of the significance of taking action, or stepping forward even when the odds seem insurmountable. But what if we, as leaders, find ourselves hindered by the weight of our own unresolved pain? What if our ability to lead with authenticity and empathy is compromised by the shadows, we carry within us?

In my pursuit of leadership, I encountered setbacks that served as stark reminders of the impact of unhealed trauma. I ventured into creating spaces for young men, driven by the desire to empower and uplift. Yet, these endeavors faltered, crippled by a lack of participation and engagement. A mentoring program, envisioned as a beacon of guidance for the youth of Liberia, struggled to take flight. And then, as if echoing the collective struggles of the world, the COVID-19 pandemic swept in, casting a dark shadow over our efforts. Amidst personal struggles and the weight of unaddressed trauma, the very ground upon which my leadership stood seemed to tremble. It was then, my dear brothers and sisters, that I realized the profound truth—that true leadership demands more than the outward façade of strength; it requires an inward journey of healing, reflection, and growth. Leadership is not solely about inspiring change in others; it is also about recognizing the need for change within us. It is about acknowledging the wounds that fester beneath the surface and taking proactive steps to address them.

The path to true leadership, my friends, is a journey that beckons us to confront our vulnerabilities and scars, and to navigate the labyrinth of our past with courage and self-awareness. As renowned author Maya Angelou wisely observed, "You may encounter many defeats, but you must not be defeated." Failure, you see, is not a mark of inadequacy; it is a steppingstone on the path to growth and transformation. Leaders of all walks have stumbled and fallen, only to rise stronger and wiser, their experiences molding them into beacons of inspiration.

Let us draw wisdom from the stories of those who have traversed the terrain of leadership, their unhealed traumas casting a shadow that led to their eventual downfall. One such story unfolds in the life of Richard Nixon, a man who rose to the highest office in the land as President of the United States. Nixon's leadership was marked by strength, determination, and yet, his unaddressed traumas seeped into his decision-making, leading to the infamous Watergate scandal. His fear of exposure, his need to prove himself, and his inability to grapple with his inner demons culminated in a crisis that rocked the nation. Nixon himself acknowledged, "I let down my friends. I let down the country. I let down our system of government and the dreams of all those young people that ought to get into government but now think it's all too corrupt and the rest."

Let us not forget the cautionary tale of Lehman Brothers, a financial giant that stood as a symbol of success and power. However, beneath the façade of prosperity lay a culture driven by unhealed traumas— pride, greed, and the insatiable hunger for more. This culture of unchecked ambition eventually led to the 2008 financial crisis, a crisis that rippled through global markets and shattered the lives of countless individuals. Dick Fuld, the CEO of Lehman Brothers, acknowledged the lessons learned too late, stating, "I wake up every single night thinking what I missed. What did I get wrong? I take this very personally." These stories, my friends, serve as mirrors that reflect the consequences of unaddressed trauma on leadership. They remind us that leadership, though noble in intent, can crumble under the weight of unresolved pain. They compel us to tread the path of self-awareness, confront our inner struggles, and acknowledge that our wounds, left unattended, can seep into every facet of our leadership.

Amidst these shadows, however, lies a glimmer of hope—a hope that emerges from the transformative power of healing. Leadership is not about wearing a mask of invulnerability; it is about embracing our authentic selves, scars and all. As the words of civil rights icon Rosa Parks remind us, "I have learned over the years that when one's mind is made up, this diminishes fear; knowing what must be done does away with fear." Acknowledging our wounds, my dear brothers and sisters is not a sign of weakness; it is an act of courage. It is an act that paves the way for personal growth, empathy, and the capacity to lead with authenticity. Just as Nelson Mandela emerged from his own trauma to become a beacon of forgiveness and reconciliation, we too can rise above the limitations of our past and forge a new path. To heal, to lead authentically, we must embrace vulnerability—the vulnerability to face our pain, to confront our demons, and to emerge stronger. It is this vulnerability that enables us to connect with others, to inspire change, and to navigate challenges with unwavering grace. As the words of Brene Brown remind us, "Vulnerability is not winning or losing; it's having the courage to show up and be seen when we have no control over the outcome."

The journey of healing, my friends, is not without its struggles. I myself, confronted by the impact of unaddressed trauma, embarked on a path of self-reflection and growth. I realized that true leadership is not a mere façade; it is a reflection of the inner work we undertake. Through self-awareness and personal responsibility, we can break free from the chains of unhealed trauma and emerge as leaders who create positive change. As leaders, we are not exempt from the struggles that plague humanity; we are part of it. Our wounds, like the scars of a battle, are reminders of our humanity, of the strength we draw from our vulnerabilities. A leader who grapples with suppressed pain is like a ship navigating treacherous waters without a rudder—directionless and adrift. However, when we take ownership of our healing, when we confront the shadows that threaten to engulf us, we chart a course toward personal growth, authenticity, and the capacity to lead with compassion.

The journey of healing, my dear brothers and sisters, requires us to delve into the depths of our souls, to confront the wounds that lie dormant, waiting to resurface. As leaders, we must be willing to seek the guidance of therapists, coaches, and mentors who can help us navigate the labyrinth of our past. Just as a skilled surgeon mends a broken bone, these professionals can guide us through the process of mending our hearts and minds. It is imperative that we learn from leaders who have faltered due to unhealed trauma. Consider the words of Steve Jobs, a visionary who transformed the world of technology. Yet, his leadership style was marred by his unresolved pain and anger, traits that strained relationships within his organization. As he reflected on his journey, Jobs noted, "My model for business is The Beatles: They were four guys that kept each other's negative tendencies in check; they balanced each other. And the total was greater than the sum of the parts. Great things in business are never done by one person, they're done by a team of people."

Leadership, my dear friends, is not a solitary endeavor; it is a symphony of collaboration, empathy, and shared purpose. Just as a conductor guides an orchestra to create harmonious music, so too must leaders navigate the complexities of their teams, acknowledging the impact of their own unhealed wounds on the collective melody. It is a journey that requires humility, a willingness to admit fault, and a commitment to healing. In the midst of my own journey, I realized that unhealed trauma can be a chain that binds us, limiting our ability to lead authentically and compassionately. It was in this moment of realization that I embarked on a path of transformation. I confronted the consequences of my own unaddressed pain—the way it had permeated my interactions, decisions, and overall effectiveness as a leader. I recognized that my tendency to mask my struggles, to put on a façade of confidence, only served to push others away. Instead of taking responsibility for my actions, I resorted to blame, adopting an approach that fractured the unity of our organization.

As I navigated these challenges, I drew strength from the lessons of leaders who have stumbled and risen anew. Consider the words of Mahatma Gandhi, a beacon of nonviolent resistance and change. His leadership was not without its struggles and failures, but he viewed these setbacks as steppingstones on the path to growth. Gandhi famously stated, "Strength does not come from physical capacity. It comes from an indomitable will." The indomitable will to confront our past, to heal, and to lead from a place of authenticity—that is the essence of true leadership. Vulnerability, my friends, is not a sign of weakness; it is a testament to our humanity. The stories of leaders who have faced adversity and emerged stronger remind us that vulnerability is the catalyst for growth and connection. The words of Theodore Roosevelt capture this sentiment eloquently: "It is not the critic who counts; not the man who points out how the strong man stumbles, or where the doer of deeds could have done them better. The credit belongs to the man who is actually in the arena, whose face is marred by dust and sweat and blood; who strives valiantly; who errs, who comes short again and again, because there is no effort without error and shortcoming."

The path to healing, my dear brothers and sisters, is a courageous journey—one that requires us to step into the arena, confront our pain, and emerge stronger and more resilient. It is a journey that demands vulnerability, authenticity, and a willingness to embrace our scars as badges of honor. Just as a phoenix rises from the ashes, so too can we rise from the depths of our pain to become leaders who inspire change and create a lasting impact. In my journey, I uncovered the profound truth that leadership is not about control or self-validation; it is about empowering, inspiring, and serving others with authenticity and vulnerability. As I grappled with the lessons of failure, I learned that leadership is a dynamic dance, a constant interplay between self-discovery and growth. It was a painful realization that my fear of vulnerability and my prideful nature hindered the very cause I sought to champion. I came to understand that leadership is not about proving ourselves; it is about uplifting others, about fostering an environment where growth, learning, and healing can flourish.

Leadership, my dear friends, is a journey that calls us to recognize our limitations and seek growth beyond them. The story of Henry Ford, a visionary in the realm of automobiles, resonates deeply. Ford faced challenges and failures that could have shattered his dreams, but he chose to view them as opportunities for growth. He famously said, "Failure is simply the opportunity to begin again, this time more intelligently." Through this lens, failure becomes a steppingstone, a chance to refine our approach and lead with renewed wisdom. The realization of our shortcomings, my dear brothers and sisters, is a testament to humility—a humility that acknowledges our imperfections and seeks growth. It was clear to me that my reluctance to be vulnerable, and my prideful stance, hindered the very purpose I yearned to fulfill. The painful experience of seeing good-hearted individuals join and then depart the organization was a clarion call for change. It was a lesson in the power of vulnerability and humility in leadership, a lesson that resonates with the words of John C. Maxwell: "A leader is one who knows the way, goes the way, and shows the way."

Let us remember, my dear friends, that leadership is not about personal glory; it is about inspiring others to reach their full potential. It is about creating a culture of growth, empathy, and resilience. Just as Martin Luther King Jr. led a movement to dismantle racial segregation, he also grappled with his own inner struggles. His leadership emerged from a wellspring of vulnerability and authenticity. As he reflected, "Darkness cannot drive out darkness; only light can do that. Hate cannot drive out hate; only love can do that." The journey of healing, my dear brothers and sisters, intertwines with the journey of those we serve. Through my non-profit organization's initiatives, we sought to empower children in underserved communities. We provided scholarships, mentorship programs, and educational resources. The impact of our work was evident in the lives of these children. They transitioned from a sense of limited opportunity to a renewed sense of hope, confidence, and resilience. Our journey together taught me that true leadership is a symphony—a harmonious dance between the leader and the led, a dance that requires vulnerability, empathy, and unwavering commitment.

But perhaps the most profound transformation occurred within me. As I witnessed lives changed and communities revitalized, I experienced a shift in perspective. Leadership, I realized, is not a pedestal of personal achievement; it is a platform for creating positive change in the lives of others. My own journey of healing became intertwined with the journey of those I served. The strength and resilience I witnessed in them fueled my own growth and transformation. It was a powerful testament to the interconnectivity of leadership, a reminder that when we lead with authenticity and compassion, our impact echoes far beyond our individual selves. Looking forward, my dear brothers and sisters, the vision of our organization is clear—a future where trauma-informed education prevails, and where every child has access to the resources and support needed to thrive. We continue to innovate, adapt, and refine our programs, driven by a commitment to address the evolving needs of the children and communities we serve. Together, we strive to create a society where trauma becomes not a barrier, but a catalyst for growth, resilience, and a brighter future for all.

The statistics, my dear friends, reveal a sobering truth—an undeniable link between unhealed trauma and leadership challenges. According to a study by the Harvard Business Review, approximately 67% of leaders have experienced traumatic events in their lives. These events can cast a long shadow, affecting decision-making, relationships, and overall effectiveness. The Center for Creative Leadership's research also highlights that suppressed trauma can lead to burnout, impaired emotional intelligence, and diminished decision-making abilities. These statistics are not a condemnation of leaders who carry trauma; rather, they underscore the importance of creating environments that foster healing and growth.

Organizations that prioritize trauma-informed practices and support systems are paving the way for leaders to heal and thrive. They recognize that healing is not a sign of weakness, but a testament to courage and resilience. These organizations provide resources such as therapy, coaching, and mentorship programs, acknowledging that leadership is a journey of constant evolution. Just as a gardener tends to a garden to ensure its growth and vitality, so too must organizations tend to the well-being of their leaders.

The impact of leaders with unhealed trauma extends beyond the individual—it permeates the organizational culture. Studies have shown that organizations led by individuals with suppressed trauma experience higher turnover rates, reduced employee satisfaction, and decreased productivity. The toxicity that stems from unaddressed trauma corrodes trust, engendering an environment of fear and disengagement. But let us not forget that these statistics are not a decree; they are a call to action. They remind us of the urgency to create environments that foster healing and growth. They compel us to embrace vulnerability, to prioritize self-awareness, and to champion personal growth not as a luxury, but as an essential component of effective leadership.

My dear brothers and sisters, let us remember that leadership is not a journey we undertake alone. It is a journey of shared growth, of mutual upliftment. Just as a tree's branches intertwine, reaching toward the sky as one unified entity, so too must leaders support and elevate one another. As the Dalai Lama wisely said, "Our prime purpose in this life is to help others. And if you can't help them, at least don't hurt them." The journey toward healing, my friends, is a journey of compassion—for ourselves and for others. It is a journey that reminds us that we are not defined by our scars, but by the way we rise above them. The stories of leaders who have faced the abyss of failure, only to emerge stronger and wiser, testify to the transformative power of healing. The words of Maya Angelou echo in our hearts: "You may not control all the events that happen to you, but you can decide not to be reduced by them."

Let us, my dear brothers and sisters, be the torchbearers of change. Let us be the leaders who acknowledge our wounds and embrace the journey of healing. Let us lead with authenticity, vulnerability, and unwavering dedication to the well-being of all. As leaders, we have the power to inspire, to uplift, and to create lasting change. Let us chart a new paradigm of leadership—one characterized by empathy, resilience, and the extraordinary impact that we can have when we lead from a place of wholeness. The path to becoming exceptional leaders, my dear friends, begins with self-awareness, empathy, and a commitment to healing. Just as a butterfly emerges from its cocoon, transformed and resplendent, so too can we emerge from the cocoon of our past, ready to spread our wings and create ripples of positive change. Let us rise above the limitations of unhealed trauma, unlocking our full potential and illuminating the path toward a world where leadership is characterized by compassion, understanding, and an unwavering dedication to the well-being of all.

Leaders are healers because they help others feel better and solve problems. But sometimes, they forget to take care of themselves. This can make their journey harder and shorter. It's important for leaders to heal themselves first before helping others. Everything they think, feel, and do affects many people, so it's crucial for them to work on themselves.

Embarking on the path of leadership requires a sturdy foundation within oneself. Without it, it's easy to become disoriented along the way. As leaders, and those aspiring to lead, it's often the case that we grapple with the pain of guiding others while struggling to lead ourselves. We find ourselves wrestling with the journey of healing, often donning the worn shoes of leadership: battered yet leading, confused yet leading. Sometimes, we find success, but more often than not, we fall short, questioning those around us and shifting blame onto others due to our own unresolved wounds and the invisible weight of past trauma holding us back.

I often ponder: can I lead and heal simultaneously? The truth is, most of us are leading and healing on a daily basis. Leadership is accompanied by cuts, bruises, scars, and tears, and on this arduous path, healing becomes an integral part of the process. However, too often, we are hurting without even recognizing the depth of our pain or acknowledging the scars left behind by past hurts. We unknowingly carry these burdens forward, leaving a trail of decisions tainted by our unresolved past.

In the words of author and trauma expert Bessel van der Kolk, 'Traumatized people chronically feel unsafe inside their bodies: The past is alive in the form of gnawing interior discomfort.' As leaders, it is imperative that we confront our past traumas and tend to our own wounds before we can effectively guide others towards healing and growth. Only then can we truly lead from a place of strength, empathy, and authenticity, paving the way for a brighter future for ourselves and those we lead. Dealing with your own past pain is a big part of getting ready to lead. If you don't, it can still affect you and how you lead. As Simon Sinek says, facing the truth now is better than lying to yourself later. Success feels good, but it's not everything. Focusing only on success can make you lose sight of who you are. True success is about more than just winning—it's about feeling good inside and being balanced. By being aware of themselves, leaders can understand how their past pain shapes them. By facing and dealing with this pain, they can grow and become even better leaders. Success isn't just about one person—it's about everyone, and it starts with knowing yourself and being strong.

CHAPTER 11

Rising Above Injustice

A Journey Of Resilience And Redemption

T erence McKenna's profound words, "Chaos is what we've lost touch with. Therefore, it is given a bad name. It is feared by the dominant archetype of our world, which is the Ego, which clenches because its existence is defined in terms of control, that echo through the corridors of our lives, especially when we consider the trials faced by individuals within our complex and often unforgiving legal system." In my journey of volunteering at a humble soup kitchen, I was privileged to meet an extraordinary individual who shared a story of unwavering resilience in the face of daunting adversity. This encounter illuminated the very essence of the chaos that Terence McKenna spoke of – a chaos that society tends to shun and fear. It is chaos inherent in the struggles of those who find themselves entangled within the legal labyrinth, a realm where uncertainty and control dance an intricate tango. In this realm, the ego often tightens its grip, clinging to a semblance of authority, for it thrives on the illusion of control.

The story of the person I met at the soup kitchen serves as a testament to the human spirit's capacity to defy this dominant archetype. It is a narrative of endurance, resilience, and the pursuit of justice amidst the cacophony of chaos. As I listened to this individual's account, I couldn't help but be reminded of the teachings of faith and perseverance that Bishop TD Jakes has imparted to countless souls seeking hope in the face of life's tumultuous storms. In the coming paragraphs, I will share this remarkable story, highlighting the strength and determination that can emerge when one confronts chaos head-on, seeking not domination but justice, not control but truth. This story is a testament to the power of the human spirit to rise above adversity and, in doing so, illuminate the path toward a more just and compassionate society.

Amid the backdrop of serving the homeless and cleansing the debris that littered the streets, I found myself in the company of a young man, much like me in age and stature, hailing from the rich tapestry of African descent. His story, a profound testament to resilience, unfolded in the shadow of a daunting legal labyrinth, one that tested his mettle in ways he could never have foreseen.

This young man's odyssey embarked upon an ordinary day, marred by an unfortunate accident involving his car, a vehicle driven by another individual. Driven by the simple desire to restore his beloved automobile, he reluctantly placed a call to the police, unknowingly setting in motion a series of events that would, in due course, challenge him to the very core of his being.

Unbeknownst to him, this solitary act would lead him to confront the formidable Assistant District Attorney (ADA) tasked with prosecuting his case. The charges laid before him were a heavy burden to bear, a weighty ten in total, each carrying its own gravity. Among these accusations were the ominous charges of leaving the scene of an accident, violating marked lanes, driving with negligence, larceny exceeding $250, and even the dire allegation of filing a false insurance claim. The enormity of these charges would have been enough to shatter the resolve of most, yet this young man stood unyielding, a symbol of unwavering determination. His journey is a parable of resilience, a testament to the human spirit's capacity to rise above adversity, and a shining example of courage in the face of chaos.

Initially overwhelmed by the sheer magnitude of the criminal charges looming over him, he confessed to harboring a profound fear of the many potential outcomes that lay ahead. The weight of his circumstances was not lost upon him, and rather than succumb to despair, he chose a path less traveled—a path illuminated by the beacon of self-education, with the singular goal of defending himself against the looming storm. As the first day of court proceedings dawned, he found himself sitting amidst a sea of uncertainty. However, a glimmer of hope pierced through the clouds of doubt when he witnessed the Assistant District Attorney (ADA) casually dismissing cases akin to his own. It was a moment that fueled the flickering flames of optimism within his heart, suggesting the possibility of a favorable resolution to his own legal ordeal.

Yet, this ember of hope would soon face a formidable trial of its own. When he approached the ADA and earnestly shared his side of the story, he was met not with understanding or compassion, but with a dismissive smirk—a gesture that seemed to mock his vulnerability. This act of indifference, a callous disregard for his predicament, struck a chord within him. It awakened a fierce determination, a resolve to champion his own cause, regardless of the odds stacked against him. Determined to represent himself in court, he made this audacious choice despite the derisive laughter that echoed through the courtroom, with the ADA leading the chorus. He became a spectacle, a target for ridicule, and yet, his spirit remained unbroken. His journey was a testament to the power of unwavering faith in oneself, a story that would inspire all who bore witness to the unfolding drama within the hallowed halls of justice. There are moments when one stands at a crossroads, their very destiny hanging in the balance. Such a pivotal juncture was faced by an individual who dared to tread the path less taken, wrestling with the decision to represent himself in the hallowed halls of justice. His choice, as profound as it was daring, would unleash a cascade of consequences that would test the very limits of his courage. The backdrop of this remarkable tale unfurled in the Commonwealth of Massachusetts, where larceny charges loomed ominously over him like a shadowy specter. These weren't mere misdemeanors; they were felonies, crimes that carried the weight of life-altering implications. As the hours on the clock dwindled, he found himself standing on the precipice of a perilous journey, one that could ultimately lead to his downfall and impact his family. The specter of never again embracing his beloved children gnawed at his heart.

Intriguingly, his apprehension about embracing the mantle revealed a profound conviction that transcended borders. He believed that his true calling and the magnitude of his impact were destined to unfold in his homeland, in ways he had yet to fathom. Yet, undaunted by the looming storm, he embarked on a quest for knowledge and wisdom. In the depths of research, he stumbled upon a book, a beacon of guidance in the darkness, written by none other than Gerry Spence, a luminary among criminal defense lawyers. Within the pages of Spence's masterpiece, he unearthed a treasure trove of insights into the intricate dance of courtroom tactics.

Spence's teachings, akin to the gospel for the seeker of justice, lit the way forward like a beacon of hope in the dark abyss. They reverberated deep within his soul, particularly the profound triad of fear, time, and evidence, which were, in Spence's wisdom, strategic layers employed to intimidate and subdue the defendant in the fierce battle for vindication. Inspired by Spence's revelation that the courtroom was not merely a stage for legal combat but a psychological arena where lawyers and the Assistant District Attorney played intricate mind games with the defendant, he embarked on a noble quest to unveil his true essence. Following Spence's sage counsel to make the legal practitioners truly see him, he set about crafting a narrative that would not only tug at their intellect but also resonate with the depths of their hearts.

With an indomitable spirit, he meticulously wove his narrative tapestry, composing an eloquent letter that cast a brilliant spotlight on his impeccable moral character, his unwavering commitment to the pursuit of academic excellence, and, above all else, his sacred duty as a devoted parent. He presented a copy of this heartfelt missive, a testament to his sincerity and unwavering resolve, to both the presiding judge and the Assistant District Attorney. At the next hearing, he strode into the courtroom, each step echoed with the resonance of destiny. The air was charged with anticipation, a palpable tension that hung between the pillars of justice. Armed with Spence's wisdom and his own unwavering belief, he stood ready to face the crucible of the legal system, fortified by the knowledge that his narrative held the power to sway hearts, minds, and perhaps, the very course of his fate.

He reported sitting outside the courtroom and looking at the ADA's shock which was palpable when he saw the defendant standing tall, armed with beating him at his own game. ADA standing in his grey 3-piece tuxedo seem disappointed. He reported sitting 15 feet away from the ADA as he dismissed multiple cases which appeared to be in anger he had been beaten at his own game. As the ADA dismissed several cases before him, his pompous demeanor gradually waned, replaced by a sense of defeat. Finally, the ADA called him, but this time, the tables had turned. He said he stood brimming with confidence and maintained unwavering eye contact, a testament to his newfound confidence. Before sitting next to the ADA, he saw the pink slip the ADA had given to others before him who left with a smile on their faces. He observed as the ADA begrudgingly wrote the dismissal of the case on a pink slip, unable to hide his disappointment at being outplayed, he sulked, with his eyes down and stated, "I saw your letter, I am going to do you a favor."

In the grand theater of life, most would have taken their leave at that victorious moment, content with their conquest. But for him, the story was far from over. He refused to let a single event define the contours of his consciousness. In a moment of remarkable candor, he chose to unburden his soul to the Assistant District Attorney (ADA), confessing to the falsehood that had shrouded his involvement in the accident. He openly admitted that he had lied to the police officers, acknowledging his guilt in a bid to obtain an insurance benefit. He sought not only to confess his transgression but to make amends by offering to pay restitution fees.

With a heart laid bare, he beseeched the ADA for pre-trial probation and an opportunity to right the wrongs he had committed. It was a moment of vulnerability and redemption, a testament to his unwavering commitment to honesty, even in the face of potential consequences. However, the ADA, still ensnared by his own ego, responded with cold indifference. He rose from his seat with an air of entitlement, proclaiming with hubris, "You will regret lying to me." In the midst of this tense exchange, an intriguing question arose: Why was he so remarkably composed in a moment that could have unraveled the very fabric of his life? His answer revealed a deep well of resilience within him. He explained that his calm demeanor stemmed from the realization that the ADA lacked substantial evidence to secure a conviction. Yet, despite this glimmer of hope, uncertainty loomed large, casting a shadow over his path.

Undaunted by the uncertain terrain ahead, he retreated into the world of knowledge, immersing himself in research and introspection. His quest for justice led him to make a pivotal decision—to seek the assistance of a court-appointed lawyer, even though he knew they were often burdened with overwhelming caseloads. With his newfound wisdom, he chose to adopt the principles of Sun Tzu's, concealing his knowledge and bestowing credit upon others. Guided by these ancient principles of wisdom, he retained a court-appointed lawyer and discreetly instructed them to pursue pretrial probation, a path of redemption that would allow him to cleanse his conscience. This marked a turning point in his journey, where the pursuit of truth and the desire for personal growth merged into a resolute commitment to face the consequences of his actions with dignity and integrity.

In the annals of his journey, he reflected upon the moment he began to question the impulsiveness of his decision. While Sun Tzu's principles of deception and strategy were brilliant, he came to realize that his own life hung precariously in the balance, along with the futures of his beloved children. His decision had been made in haste, fueled by emotion, and he grappled with the realization that he had gambled everything on this impulsive choice.

Despite the fear that coursed through his veins and the uncertainty that clouded his thoughts, a remarkable calmness settled over him whenever he ventured into the intimidating domain of the courthouse. He attributed this composure to a profound insight - a glimpse of defeat etched on the ADA's face. It was as if the sands of time were slipping away from the prosecutor's grasp, and the inevitable dismissal of the case loomed on the horizon.

The ADA, shaken and bewildered by the turn of events, couldn't contain his curiosity. He probed the court-appointed lawyer about the defendant's seemingly encyclopedic knowledge of legal strategies. The lawyer, wise as a sage, simply attributed it to guidance received from another seasoned attorney.

As the judicial saga unfolded over numerous court appearances, employing their customary psychological tactics, and attempting to wear down the resolve of the vulnerable, he remained undaunted. He sat through every hearing, his spirit unwavering, driven by a singular purpose: to cleanse his conscience and seek redemption. After more than four arduous court dates, the inevitable occurred— the case was finally set for trial.

As the trial commenced, the ADA found himself unable to substantiate his claims. Faced with the stark reality of a crumbling case, he struck a deal with the court-appointed lawyer. The terms were clear: payment of restitution fees and placement on pre-trial probation. Victory, hard-fought and well-earned, had been achieved through the very system that once seemed daunting.

In retrospect, he offered profound insights into the lessons he had gleaned from his erratic decision-making. He recognized that his impulsive choices could have easily derailed his life and wreaked havoc on his family's well-being. It was this recognition that fueled his desire to share this remarkable story. When asked why he was sharing this narrative, he revealed his motivation. He saw a reflection of himself in others, particularly in those navigating the complex labyrinth of the American legal system, especially as a black man. He understood that the courtroom could be an intimidating and unforgiving place, where fear often held sway. However, he passionately believed that with knowledge, research, and a fundamental understanding of the legal landscape, individuals could gain the confidence to stand unwaveringly before the judge.

In the resounding echoes of his journey, this young man courageously unveiled the harsh realities faced by people of color within the intricate web of the criminal justice system. He discovered that the scales of justice, despite their claim to impartiality, often carried a bias that belied their blindfolded facade. In this labyrinth of legal intricacies, truth-telling frequently incurred punishment, while deceit was lauded and rewarded. The path he trod was strewn with sadness and despair, yet his unwavering faith in the absence of evidence against him served as an unyielding beacon, guiding him through the darkest of storms.

His story emerges as a powerful testament, reminding us that amidst the chaos and complexities of the legal realm, individuals harbor the capacity to advocate for themselves and conquer seemingly insurmountable odds. He recounted how he became ensnared in a convoluted web of charges stemming from an accident that was not of his making. As a person of color, he keenly observed the disparities embedded within the system. His observations align with the findings of research, which lay bare a disconcerting pattern of wrongful convictions and bias against minorities and foreign-born individuals within the criminal justice system. The Innocence Project, in its study, revealed that minorities, particularly African Americans, bore a disproportionate burden of wrongful convictions when compared to their white counterparts. Immigrants and refugees, facing unique challenges, often traverse the legal labyrinth without the resources and support necessary for their defense.

Dr. Maria Martinez, a trauma specialist, underscores the profound impact of such injustices on individuals. She notes, "Being wrongfully convicted and subjected to unfair treatment within the court system can inflict severe emotional and psychological trauma. It erodes trust in institutions and can exert long-lasting effects on one's well-being." The young man's narrative stands as a testament to the resilience that can be summoned by individuals thrust into a broken system. It underscores the pivotal importance of self-education, preparation, and the relentless pursuit of justice.

The words of George Washington resonate deeply: "The truth will ultimately prevail where there are pains to bring it to light." In the face of false accusations and a flawed justice system, those wrongly convicted have demonstrated remarkable resilience. Their stories resonate with the conviction that truth cannot remain concealed indefinitely. These individuals have weathered immense trials but have emerged with unshakable resolve, determined to reclaim their innocence and restore justice. One among them, who navigated the labyrinthine court system, shared his experience, stating, "I was deemed guilty before being afforded a fair chance to prove my innocence. It was a bleak period, but I refused to be defined by that darkness."

Despite the formidable challenges they confronted, these individuals have emerged with a profound sense of resilience and a fervent commitment to catalyze change. They have become beacons of hope and staunch advocates for a more equitable legal system. Their stories illuminate the shadows, exposing the system's flaws, and inspire others to demand reform. Their journeys are a testament to the potency of determination and the indomitable human spirit.

Nelson Mandela's words resound: "It always seems impossible until it's done." The path to justice may be strewn with obstacles, but it is not insurmountable. With unwavering determination and a collective effort, we can strive toward a more just and equitable society. We must heed the words of Dr. Martin Luther King Jr.: "Injustice anywhere is a threat to justice everywhere." In the face of adversity, our true character is unveiled, and through collective endeavor, we can reshape the narrative of justice. Together, let us strive for a world where the innocent are safeguarded, the guilty are held accountable, and the principles of truth and fairness guide every courtroom.

In the eloquent words of Terence McKenna, "Chaos is what we've lost touch with." Let us embrace that chaos, rekindling the potential for change and transformation. Together, we can reshape the legal landscape, forging a path where truth ultimately prevails and justice unequivocally triumphs. Amidst the challenges, we shall find our strength, and in the collective journey toward justice, we shall discover our enduring legacy. Regardless of our race, let us seek truth not merely in words but in the wisdom gleaned from thorough research, piercing through biases that even the courts may harbor.

As a black man navigating within this system, I've witnessed the injustices faced by many who share my skin color. It's perplexing and disheartening to see individuals targeted, often solely because of their complexion. When one voice speaks of injustice, it demands attention, but when countless voices echo the same plight, it calls for systemic evaluation. We must acknowledge those within the justice system who tirelessly strive for fairness. Yet, it's undeniable that data shows a prejudicial tilt against Black individuals. The system, run by flawed humans, exhibits biases that inflict wounds akin to tattoo needles upon our souls. I think of my cousin, his smile radiant, his confidence unwavering, his grace regal—cut down tragically, his killer still at large. Justice eludes us, and I witness my aunt's anguish daily, her steps heavy with loneliness as she seeks closure.

The system, originally designed to serve all, seems skewed to favor the privileged few, neglecting those with limited resources. History bears witness—justice often reserved for the affluent, the geographically fortunate, the fair-skinned. But let this not be a lamentation, rather a clarion call to action. With wisdom, we arm ourselves to navigate this labyrinth of bias and inequality. Knowledge is our shield, our guide to turn potential adversity into triumph. Statistics paint a stark picture: Black men disproportionately bear the brunt of the criminal justice system's injustices compared to their Caucasian counterparts. But armed with understanding and determination, we possess the power to soar above adversity, to rise like the eagle, with a vision so keen, foreseeing victory before its fruition. Remember, as the Constitution declares, the power resides within us. The challenges we face are not insurmountable; with unwavering resolve, we can transcend and conquer.

CHAPTER 12

Embracing The Power Of Fatherhood

Redefining Roles, Shaping Lives

Have you ever felt the deep bond of love with a child, only to watch it strained as the parents part ways, turning the child into a pawn in their conflicts? If so, you know the turbulent path many fathers tread, often making choices they regret, affecting their children deeply. I count myself incredibly fortunate to have grown up in a loving home, with parents who've shared over 45 years of marriage. Now, as a father to four wonderful sons, I reflect on my own upbringing. Looking back, I recognize that my very existence owes much to my father's presence. Like many fathers, my dad was far from perfect. He had his flaws and made his fair share of mistakes, but I am eternally grateful for his unwavering presence in my life. A man who chooses to stay, even when societal norms suggest otherwise, transcends the boundaries of this world. Such a man operates on a different plane, one that breaks free from the constraints of earthly dichotomies.

Psychologists tell us that children's behavior is often shaped by their environment, including the people, places, and experiences they encounter. They emphasize that the presence or absence of a father can have a profound impact on a child's life, for better or worse. Just as my father's presence guided me through both the darkest and brightest moments of my life, I've had the privilege of firsthand observation, witnessing the consequences of a father's absence on children's development.

As a dedicated social worker in the Commonwealth of Massachusetts, my primary mission is to ensure the permanency, safety, and well-being of all children. In this role, I am all too familiar with the detrimental effects of a father's absence in households. I've encountered heart-wrenching scenarios of children falling into drug abuse, becoming victims of sexual exploitation by their mothers' partners, enduring physical abuse, neglect, and abandonment, among other harrowing experiences. This is not to suggest that these problems don't occur in homes with fathers present, but the impact of a father's presence is undeniable. It provides children with a sense of security, protection, and an unwavering foundation that makes them less susceptible to negative influences from peers and their environment. Children growing up without their fathers often experience feelings of confusion, isolation, and an overwhelming sense of loneliness. These emotions can shape their struggles with identity, forming healthy relationships, making decisions, and breaking free from destructive cycles perpetuated in father-absent homes.

The power of a father is beyond human comprehension. In essence, fathers are the protectors, providers, and bearers of love for their families. It was from the love of a father that God created a woman, emphasizing the profound connection between a father's love and the creation of life itself. While I may not be a biblical scholar, my experiences as both a father and the product of a father's love have taught me that fatherhood is a complex blessing. As fathers, we must navigate the intricacies of our children's lives with the wisdom of serpents, ensuring they grow in a way that aligns with our values and the path we hope they will take. While I am deeply committed to my profession and its mission to safeguard children and families, my role as a father always takes precedence. Mahatma Gandhi's words serve as a guiding light: "The earth, the air, the land, and the water are not an inheritance from our forefathers but on loan from our children." Through my own failures and experiences as a father, I have come to realize that parenthood is simultaneously the most significant and most thankless job on this planet.

My journey into fatherhood wasn't meticulously planned, as it is for many fathers. Instead, it was born from my reluctance to confront the painful truths of my childhood. I failed to address the scars of my past, and this inability continues to cast a shadow over my adulthood. When my first son was born, I held dreams of eternal togetherness with his mother. However, after two and a half years, our relationship ended, and my love for my child was weaponized, leading to years of courtroom battles that weighed heavily on my conscience. The legal system often favored his mother, and this imbalance left me feeling powerless. My struggles with trust and love stemming from my previous relationship woes led to further complications. I found myself in a new relationship, and the result was my second child. However, the same insecurities and emotional barriers caused this relationship to crumble, primarily due to my inability to trust and be present. Currently, I am engaged to the mother of my third child, who has a son from a previous relationship. I mention these complexities to highlight how my decisions have led to multiple children born out of wedlock and, regrettably, the unintentional harm inflicted upon my children as I navigated these tumultuous relationships.

My journey is a testament to the importance of addressing mental health and past traumas. I've often jumped from one relationship to another, unintentionally causing emotional harm to my children in the process. This reflection serves as a reminder that, as fathers, we must be aware of our own emotional baggage and work towards healing it, not only for our sake but for the well-being of our children. Let us remember that fatherhood is a sacred responsibility, one that should not be undertaken lightly. It is a journey filled with complexity and challenges, but it is also a journey of growth, love, and unwavering commitment. As fathers, we must strive to break the cycle of our own past traumas, prioritizing the well-being of our children and providing them with the love, security, and guidance they need to thrive. Our presence in their lives is immeasurable, and the legacy we leave will resonate for generations to come. I am fortunate to have the opportunity to visit homes on a weekly basis, where I witness firsthand the challenges faced by children and families whose lives are in disarray due to a multitude of factors, chief among them being the absence of a father figure. We find ourselves living in a generation where, often unconsciously, we downplay the significance of fathers, and this trend has wrought havoc upon the very fabric of our family systems. The consequences of this societal perspective, rooted in the shadows of childhood trauma, have been instrumental in driving some men to surrender and abandon their homes.

It is vital to acknowledge that society's view of fathers is often molded by deeply ingrained beliefs, many of which find their origins in past traumas and experiences. These perspectives, while widely held, are nothing short of detrimental to the well-being of our families. They undermine the pivotal role fathers play in nurturing and shaping the lives of their children. This skewed perspective on fathers frequently emanates from the antiquated notion that men are the breadwinners, solely responsible for financial support, while women are expected to stay at home, tending solely to the care of their children. While this belief may still persist in various parts of the world, those of us living in the Western world have come to understand that maintaining professional careers for both parents while simultaneously upholding family standards necessitates active involvement from both mothers and fathers alike.

In this contemporary landscape, it is increasingly evident that gender roles within the family unit have evolved. The rigid dichotomy of yesteryears, where men were exclusively associated with the workforce and women confined to domestic roles, no longer accurately reflects the complexities of modern life. We have recognized that the well-rounded development of our children necessitates the active engagement of both parents. When fathers and mothers alike are wholeheartedly present in their children's lives, it contributes significantly to their mental, emotional, and physical well-being. This paradigm shift is not an affront to the traditional roles of fathers or mothers but rather a realization that the nurturing and guiding of our children require a shared responsibility. The emotional, psychological, and social development of our children thrives when both parents actively participate in their upbringing. Fathers bring a unique perspective and set of qualities to the parenting dynamic, just as mothers do. It is in the harmonious blending of these roles that we create an environment that best supports our children's growth and flourishing.

It is my sincere belief that fathers, like mothers, do not seek to be pampered; rather, they yearn to be acknowledged, heard, and recognized as equals in the parenting journey. This desire arises from a profound wellspring of emotions, shaped and molded by the experiences of our own childhoods. These experiences have a profound impact on the decisions we make as adults and the way we navigate the complexities of parenthood. Extensive research has illuminated the fact that fathers who have weathered traumatic experiences in their own lives, such as childhood abuse, neglect, or exposure to violence, often find themselves grappling with a multitude of challenges. These challenges, in turn, can have far-reaching effects on their mental health, emotional well-being, and capacity to create a safe and nurturing environment for their own children.

One notable study, published in the Journal of Family Violence, delved into the lives of fathers who had endured trauma. The findings were both eye-opening and disheartening, revealing that fathers with a history of trauma were more susceptible to engaging in abusive behaviors toward their own children. The lingering effects of the trauma they had experienced cast long shadows over their psychological well-being, disrupting their emotional equilibrium and undermining their ability to break free from the cycle of violence. These fathers, whose hearts once bore the weight of their own past suffering, found it arduous to provide the secure and loving environment that every child deserves. The impact of trauma extends beyond the confines of individual behaviors and resonates deeply within the realm of relationships, especially co-parenting dynamics. A comprehensive study conducted by the National Child Traumatic Stress Network underscores this fact, revealing that fathers who have walked the harrowing path of trauma often encounter formidable hurdles in co-parenting. These hurdles manifest in the form of communication challenges, pervasive mistrust, and the difficulty in establishing healthy boundaries. Regrettably, these factors serve to exacerbate instability and stress within the family unit, invariably taking a toll on the well-being of the children.

It is imperative that we recognize the intricate interplay between the past and the present in the lives of fathers. The scars borne from traumatic childhoods can influence not only their own psychological landscape but also the emotional terrain of their children. Thus, it becomes our collective responsibility to extend compassion, support, and understanding to fathers who have confronted the demons of their past. As we navigate the complexities of fatherhood, let us remain mindful of the profound impact that our own experiences can have on our journey as parents. It is through this awareness that we can strive to break free from the shackles of our past, foster healthy relationships with our children, and create a nurturing environment where they can thrive and flourish. The voices of fathers, resilient and unwavering, often echo in the corridors of indifference, unheard, and uncelebrated. This painful reality was starkly illustrated in my own life when I found myself entangled in a legal battle for the custody and well-being of my eldest son.

I vividly recall the moment when my eldest son's mother chose to end our relationship, leaving my son in my care. As a father, I understood that it was my solemn responsibility to nurture and protect my child. I didn't seek accolades or applause; rather, I comprehended the profound significance of my role in his life. I embarked on this journey with an unwavering commitment to provide the love and stability he needed to thrive.

However, life took an unexpected turn when, after a six-month hiatus from her son, my son's mother reappeared on the scene. Legal battles ensued, and the courtroom became the arena where our fate would be decided. To my dismay, the judge awarded her custody, setting in motion a years-long ordeal that would see my child taken out of state and even out of the country. In my quest for justice, I found myself face to face with a legal system that, all too often, leans heavily toward biases against fathers. The court's decision, predicated on the absence of physical harm, left me feeling undervalued and unheard. As a social worker, I was acutely aware of the systemic prejudices that often shape such judgments, yet experiencing this bias firsthand pierced my heart. It was a disheartening reminder of the uphill battle fathers often face when advocating for their rightful place in their children's lives.

I am immensely grateful that my oldest son has thrived, excelling in school and in life despite the turbulent early years. However, the scars of those uncertainties and court battles remain etched in my memory. My personal journey navigating the legal system underscores a sobering truth: fathers are routinely marginalized as parents; despite the critical role we play in our children's lives. In our collective journey as fathers, we grapple with the stark reality of a legal system that all too often dismisses or undermines our significance. It is a disheartening testament to the prevalence of cases where fathers' voices are silenced, and their rights are relegated to the background.

Statistics offer a stark and unflinching portrayal of the profound impact a father's absence can have on the lives of children. The U.S. Census Bureau illuminates a sobering reality: approximately one in four children in the United States grows up in a home without a father. This absence of a father figure reverberates across numerous dimensions of a child's existence, casting shadows that extend into their academic, emotional, and social spheres. Studies, conducted with unwavering consistency, have unearthed a troubling correlation: children without actively involved fathers are more susceptible to encountering a myriad of challenges. These challenges manifest academically, where children from father-absent homes often grapple with learning difficulties. Emotionally, the absence of a father figure can leave an indelible mark, making children more vulnerable to emotional turbulence and mental health issues. Socially, they may find it arduous to navigate relationships and societal norms, creating a sense of isolation and detachment.

The National Fatherhood Initiative, an organization dedicated to promoting responsible fatherhood, reports that children raised in father-absent homes are four times more likely to dwell in poverty. This harrowing statistic underscores the financial hardships that often accompany the absence of a father's support. It's a stark reminder that fathers play a pivotal role not only in providing emotional stability but also in ensuring the economic well-being of their children.

Moreover, the repercussions extend beyond financial struggles. These children face a heightened risk of behavioral problems, substance abuse, and engagement in criminal activities. The absence of a father figure leaves a void that can sometimes be filled by negative influences, pushing these children onto precarious paths. Tragically, the legal system and Child Welfare often fall short in delivering the support and protection fathers so rightfully deserve. Fathers, who earnestly seek custody or visitation rights, too frequently encounter indifference or dismissal. This perpetuates the cycle of fathers' absence, depriving children of the opportunity to cultivate meaningful relationships with their dads. In cases devoid of allegations of abuse or neglect, fathers are all too often confronted with biases and preconceived notions that erode their standing as caregivers and providers. The courts, at times, default to granting custody to the mother, discounting the invaluable contributions that fathers can make to their children's lives. This systemic bias compounds the challenges fathers face in securing their rightful place in their children's upbringing. It is crucial to acknowledge that fathers are not mere spectators in the journey of parenthood. They are essential pillars, deserving of recognition, support, and respect.

My journey as a parent is a testament to the transformative power of embracing failure, wearing one's scars as badges of wisdom, and recognizing that life's most profound lessons often emerge from the crucible of our shortcomings. I stand before you as a graduate of the School of Failure, not with regret but with gratitude for the invaluable teachings it has bestowed upon me. Through the maze of relationships, I have navigated, I have taken ownership of my role in each one that didn't endure. In the depths of my pain, my unhealed trauma inadvertently inflicted wounds upon women who sought solace in my presence. It is this very journey, fraught with missteps and self-discovery, that has endowed me with profound insights and an unwavering strength to confront my inner demons.

My gratitude for this newfound wisdom is rooted in the timeless teachings of the Bible, the scriptures, and the sage counsel imparted by my father. He instilled in me the unshakable belief that women are not to bear the blame when a home shatters or a child's life takes an unforeseen turn. I am not alluding to the heinous transgressions committed by either partner. Instead, I emphasize the pivotal role that men play, starting from the moment their gaze meets that of a young lady. God, in His divine wisdom, created man first, bestowing upon him the responsibilities of protection, love, and provision. It falls upon every man's shoulder to earnestly endeavor to fulfill these sacred duties. In a world where societal norms are evolving, and women are increasingly empowered in various spheres, the onus rests on men to rise above antiquated expectations and embrace their evolving roles. The strength of a family unit lies in the harmonious collaboration of both parents, irrespective of their financial contributions.

We must be hungry for self-improvement, unwavering in our commitment to providing for our families, and steadfast in our love and protection. As fathers, we must model positive attributes for our children, as espoused in the Bible verse that urges us to "Train a child in a way that when he goes, he will not depart from it." Reflecting upon my own upbringing, I realize that my father, though a well-intentioned man, was seldom vocal about imparting the tools and skills necessary for parenting. He bore the weight of his own unresolved traumas, which cast a shadow over our emotional connection. Consequently, I found myself navigating the treacherous waters of fatherhood largely in solitude, learning the ropes through trial and error.

I am haunted by the memories of heated arguments and hurtful words exchanged with my eldest son's mother. My tumultuous journey led me to a path of seeking solace in fleeting relationships, a futile quest to find within others what I desperately needed to discover within myself. These acts of selfishness reverberated through my life, serving as painful reminders of my past experiences. The echoes of my own childhood trauma emerged, unbidden, at unexpected moments, igniting bouts of anxiety and self-doubt. It has been an arduous journey to shed the emotional baggage that hinders me from openly expressing affection and providing unwavering emotional support to my son. I grapple with a deep-seated fear of perpetuating the patterns of emotional distance that characterized my relationship with my own father and the lasting impact it had on me.

Yet, this journey of self-discovery is not one of desolation but of resilience. It is a testament to the human capacity for growth, healing, and transformation. Through these trials, I have emerged as a father who is more aware, more compassionate, and more committed to breaking free from the cycle of generational trauma.

My determination remains unwavering, fueled by the unwavering desire to provide my sons with a nurturing and stable environment, where they can freely express their emotions and find validation in their feelings. Each day, I strive to communicate openly with them, sharing my own vulnerabilities and imperfections, so they understand that making mistakes and not having all the answers are natural aspects of life. My journey is one of continuous learning, as I work to address past trauma, navigate the unpredictable currents of emotions, and, most importantly, be the steadfast and loving father my sons need. In my story, I find solace in the knowledge that we, as fathers, are not defined by our past but by our commitment to shaping a brighter future for our children, one filled with love, understanding, and unwavering support.

As fathers, we hold a crucial role in shaping our children's lives. Recently, I found myself confronted with a challenging situation involving my stepson, a third grader who had been labeled as hyperactive and behaviorally challenged. Despite my background in clinical psychology, I chose to observe quietly as my fiancée discussed evaluating him with the school. When I eventually joined the conversation, their surprise was evident - they hadn't anticipated a father figure being involved. As they detailed my son's behaviors, I couldn't help but notice a pattern of typical third-grade conduct, yet they seemed fixated on the notion of evaluation.

Respectfully, I probed their perspective, questioning whether my son was the sole student exhibiting such behaviors this year. Each time, they dismissed it as irrelevant. I sensed bias creeping into the conversation, particularly when they appeared taken aback by my presence as the father figure. My fiancée and I were adamant about not allowing them to proceed with an evaluation based solely on behaviors, fully aware of the biases that can adversely affect black students within the school system. Drawing from my experiences at the multicultural wellness center, I underscored the importance of setting biases aside. As a psychologist, I've witnessed how biases can seep into counseling and teaching, resulting in unfair treatment for students who don't conform to societal expectations. I made it unequivocally clear that our son would not undergo evaluation for behaviors that did not impact his academic performance. With my fiancée standing by my side, we left that meeting knowing we had staunchly defended our son's rights.

Contemplating my own upbringing, I'm profoundly moved by the weight of fatherhood's significance. It transcends mere biological ties; it embodies the courage to nurture and guide our children in a world fraught with challenges. In the poignant words of former President Barack Obama, 'Any fool can have a child. That doesn't make you a father. It's the courage to raise a child that makes you a father. As fathers, our presence is indispensable. Whether it's sitting through school meetings, holding their hand at doctor visits, or cheering them on at sports events, our active involvement leaves an enduring mark. Even when our efforts may seem overlooked, through our steadfast sacrifices, we express an unwavering devotion to our children. Let us be reminded of the profound impact we have as fathers, not just in the lives of our children but in shaping the future generation. May we continue to embrace the responsibility with courage, love, and an unwavering commitment to their well-being.

CHAPTER 13

Embracing The Journey

Overcoming Blame And Finding Healing

W e are indeed born into a world where the possibility of failure looms, and oftentimes, it is our fear of failure that holds us back from reaching our true potential. Life is a tapestry woven with threads of uncertainty, and in this, we can find a certain kind of certainty. It is a certainty that reminds us of our imperfections, of the fragility of our existence— here today, gone tomorrow. We are, in our essence, broken and incomplete, and it is this very imperfection that makes us beautifully human. In our pursuit of an elusive perfection, we often overlook the simple truth that life's challenges and indecencies are, in fact, its essence. It is through these challenges that we grow, learn, and evolve. It is through our imperfections and struggles that we discover the strength within us to overcome adversity.

Yes, my dear brothers and sisters, we must recognize that life's journey is not a straight path free of obstacles; it is a winding road with bumps and detours along the way. But it is also a journey filled with blessings and successes that emerge from the very failures we encounter. Each setback is an opportunity to learn, to adapt, and to grow stronger. Each failure is a steppingstone toward a greater understanding of ourselves and the world around us. It is in our moments of vulnerability and humility that we find the courage to rise above our fears and continue our journey. Let us not be disheartened by the inevitability of failure, but rather, let us embrace it as a companion on our path to self-discovery and personal growth. Let us remember that our imperfections are what make us unique, and our resilience in the face of failure is what makes us truly remarkable.

In the intricate tapestry of our lives, we inevitably encounter trauma, pain, suffering, and loneliness. It is part of the human condition, a shared experience that transcends boundaries and backgrounds. It is all too common to seek scapegoats for the tribulations we face— pointing fingers at our parents, siblings, or significant others, holding them responsible for the burdens we carry. While it is undeniable that malevolent individuals exist in the world, individuals whose actions can profoundly impact our mental and emotional well-being, it is essential that we find the strength to rise above the shadows of blame and resentment.

Living in the past, perpetually fixated on the wrongs done to us and ensnared by blame, is like imprisoning ourselves in a stagnant time that refuses to evolve or change. It is a self-imposed sentence that robs us of the beauty and potential of the present moment. We may have valid reasons to feel anger, resentment, or blame for the injustices we've endured—whether it's the pain inflicted by abusive relationships, the absence of a loving parent, or any other source of suffering. These emotions are natural responses to wrongs committed against us, and they are part of our human experience. However, holding onto blame for the past serves only to corrode our present and poison our future. As we navigate the intricate tapestry of life, we must recognize that the power to shape our destinies resides within us. It begins with acknowledging the pain and injustices we've faced, understanding their impact on our lives, and making a conscious choice to transcend them.

Forgiveness, my dear friends, is not an act of condoning or forgetting the wrongs committed against us. It is a profound gift we give to ourselves—a gift of liberation from the chains of resentment and anger that bind us to the past. Through forgiveness, we unburden our hearts and minds, creating space for healing, growth, and transformation. We become the architects of our own narratives, reclaiming the power to shape our futures rather than remaining prisoners of our past. In this journey of life, let us remember that we are not defined by the wounds we bear or the injustices we've suffered. We are defined by our resilience, our capacity for forgiveness, and our ability to rise above adversity. My dear brothers and sisters, let us heed the call to release blame and embrace the present with open hearts. Let us recognize that the past does not hold the power to define our worth or determine our future. Instead, it is in our capacity to forgive and let go that we find the key to unlocking the boundless potential of the here and now.

For a significant stretch of time, I found myself entangled in a web of resentment towards my parents, holding them solely responsible for the traumatic ordeals that defined my tumultuous childhood. These painful memories included the haunting specter of sexual abuse, the despair of homelessness, the gnawing ache of hunger, the heart-wrenching abandonment, and the excruciating loss of beloved family and friends. Each of these experiences left indelible scars on my psyche, and I couldn't help but direct my anger and blame towards the very people who were meant to protect and nurture me.

I recalled reconnecting with my parents after three years of separation. Strangely, the very individuals who should have been familiar and comforting appeared as distant strangers, hailing from an unfamiliar land. The weight of blame and bitterness that I had carried within, akin to an anchor, had transformed into an all-encompassing burden that pressed down upon me. This heavy emotional load mirrored the profound chasm that had grown and festered due to their absence and the harrowing pain I endured. I held on to that resentment and became entangled in my own webs of isolation and separation which later impacted the way I socialized and connected with others. This stubborn inability to disentangle myself from the clutches of resentment obstructed not only my personal progress but also hindered my capacity to embrace the vital process of healing. It was as if I had become ensnared in a cycle of bitterness, preventing me from moving forward, from mending the shattered pieces of my soul. The wounds ran deep, and they held me captive in a state of perpetual turmoil, obscuring the path to reconciliation and personal growth.

Yet, within the shadows of despair, I began to glimpse the faint flicker of hope. The realization dawned that the burden of resentment was not just borne by me alone; My inability to disentangle myself from the relentless clutches of resentment had repercussions that extended far beyond my own well-being. It was a formidable obstacle not only to my personal progress but also to my capacity to embrace the healing that I so desperately needed. I found myself trapped in a seemingly inescapable web of emotions; a web intricately woven by the painful memories of the past. This entanglement hindered my forward momentum, shackling me to the past and preventing me from moving toward the peace and recovery I so earnestly sought.

The repercussions of placing the entire weight of blame squarely upon my parents' shoulders reverberated deeply within the intricate contours of my mental and emotional well-being. This ill-fated choice carved a perilous path leading me into the treacherous terrains of anxiety, the seemingly bottomless abyss of depression, and an overwhelming sense of personal inadequacy. The wounds inflicted by the harrowing past appeared to fester incessantly, casting an ominous and insurmountable shadow over any potential for personal growth or the pursuit of happiness.

Within this internal conflict, I found myself gravitating towards forming relationships with individuals whose life choices were questionable, a consequence of my eroded sense of trust in the world. These decisions, influenced by my festering resentment and emotional turmoil, set in motion a chain of repercussions that rippled through every aspect of my life. They left their mark on my academic pursuits, where my focus and ambition faltered, and at home, where the atmosphere grew increasingly strained.

This chain of events reached its crescendo in a cycle of physical abuse, a deeply painful and damaging manifestation of the unresolved turmoil I carried within. The physical abuse only added more layers to the festering mound of resentment that had already taken root in my heart. In this sequence of blame and pain, the vicious cycle only perpetuated more suffering, creating a self-destructive pattern that seemed impossible to break free from. The weight of blame and resentment bore down on my shoulders, pushing me onto a dark and treacherous path. It was a path where I found myself gravitating towards cliques and gangs that dabbled in the dangerous world of drug dealing and substance abuse. I played with the emotions of others, treating them callously as if changing the channel on a TV, unaware of the harm I inflicted. I recklessly engaged in a myriad of risk-taking behaviors, some so perilous that I shudder to even speak of them, knowing they could have easily led me into the deepest abyss. With every poor decision, I felt the isolation of loneliness wrapping itself around me like a suffocating shroud. It seemed as though I was imprisoned by the choices I had made, and the chains of my past grew heavier with each passing day. The path I walked was fraught with danger, and I knew that I needed to find a way out before it was too late.

In a transformative moment, born out of sheer desperation for change, I summoned an unwavering resolve to break free from the suffocating chains of victimhood and ceaseless finger-pointing. It was an epiphany that would reshape the course of my life. I sought refuge in the wisdom and guidance offered by friends and virtual mentors who had traversed similar tumultuous journeys. Among these luminaries were the likes of Bishop TD Jakes, Apostle Joshua Selman, the motivational powerhouse Les Brown, and the sage of self-improvement, Tony Robbins. Their words of wisdom served as beacons in the darkness, illuminating a path toward personal transformation and growth.

Yet, the guidance of these mentors was not my sole source of enlightenment. A treasure trove of books also accompanied me on this profound journey of self-discovery. With each page I turned, I gleaned invaluable insights that gradually shifted my perspective. Instead of lingering in the painful wounds of the past, I began to forge a new path towards healing and self-empowerment. The wellsprings of my emotions found solace in creative outlets, with writing emerging as a powerful vessel to channel the turmoil that had long been suppressed within me. The act of journaling, or pouring out my raw feelings onto paper, became a cathartic endeavor that allowed me to gradually chip away at the immense burden I had carried for so long. It was through these written words that I found a sense of release, a means to untangle the complex web of emotions that had ensnared me. Each word I penned became a steppingstone on my path to reclaiming my agency and reshaping my own narrative.

Crucially, a profound revelation crystallized within me like a glistening gem: my parents were not the sole architects of the intricate tapestry of my life. They, like all of us, were mere mortals navigating their own turbulent battles and limitations, unwittingly shaping their decisions through the lens of their personal struggles.

This newfound perspective allowed me to extend a compassionate hand toward them, not to absolve their actions, but to grasp the intricate complexity of their lives. It was an understanding that breathed empathy into my heart, illuminating the multifaceted layers of their humanity. With this empathetic understanding as my compass, I found myself gradually unburdened from the oppressive yoke of blame that had weighed me down for so long. The pivotal act of forgiveness emerged as a beacon of transformation in my journey. It was a recognition that forgiveness wasn't about condoning or justifying their actions; rather, it was a powerful vehicle for emancipating myself from the relentless clutches of the past. It was a profound release that allowed me to relinquish the past's grip on my present and future. In this transformative journey, I came to understand that forgiveness was an intricate thread intricately woven into the fabric of my healing and growth. It became a potent means through which I could reclaim my agency and craft a narrative that was no longer tethered to the shadows of the past. With each step forward, I realized that forgiveness was not a sign of weakness but a testament to my resilience and my capacity to rise above the pain, forging a future that was shaped by my choices and not the scars of the past.

This newfound sense of self-compassion was not an instantaneous revelation, but rather a gradual unfurling, like the petals of a flower opening to the sun. I began to recognize the unrelenting harshness with which I had judged myself over the years. The mistakes and shortcomings that I had mercilessly scrutinized started to take on a different hue – one that was softer, more understanding, and rooted in the understanding that growth often emerged from the fertile soil of imperfection. As I let the gentle currents of self-compassion flow through me, I realized that it was not an act of self-indulgence or a way to absolve myself from responsibility. Rather, it was a profound acknowledgment of my own humanity, a recognition that the journey of self-improvement was not about striving for some unattainable state of flawlessness, but about nurturing a relationship with myself that was grounded in kindness and understanding.

With time, this realization fostered a remarkable transformation within me. The harsh inner critic that had once held dominion over my thoughts began to recede, making space for a more benevolent and understanding voice. I started to approach my challenges and setbacks with a renewed sense of gentleness, understanding that these were not reflections of my worth but simply steppingstones on the path of growth. The concept of self-compassion wasn't confined to mere philosophical understanding; it manifested tangibly in my actions. I began to prioritize self-care and self-nurturing activities, not as acts of selfishness, but as essential components of maintaining my overall well-being. This transition allowed me to cultivate a sense of balance and harmony, nurturing not just my emotional and mental realms but also my physical self. Nurturing my inner child became essential for healing and moving forward. Embracing my past as part of my journey, rather than letting it define me, opened the door to self-discovery and a deeper understanding of who I truly was. I recognized my strength, resilience, and capacity for love and compassion. Instead of defining myself by my past traumas, I embraced the journey of healing as an integral part of my identity.

As we continue our journey of healing and self-discovery, it's crucial to acknowledge that trauma and blame are not isolated experiences. According to UNICEF, millions of children around the world suffer from various forms of trauma, and they often face blame from different sources, including loved ones and caregivers. However, we must remember that our past does not have to define us, and our focus should be on embracing the present while acknowledging the past as a part of our journey. In the face of trauma and pain, it can be tempting to give up on life. As Bishop TD Jakes, once said, "You may have had unfair things happen to you, but the depth of your pain is an indication of the height of your future." These words remind us that our pain can be a catalyst for growth and resilience. Instead of allowing trauma and blame to consume us, we must harness our experiences as steppingstones toward a brighter future.

Apostle Joshua Selman, a luminary in the realm of spiritual leadership, stands as a beacon of insight, guiding us toward the profound realms of self-acceptance and forgiveness. His teachings echo like gentle ripples across the vast expanse of human consciousness, imparting timeless wisdom that transcends boundaries and resonates deeply within the chambers of our hearts. One such gem of wisdom he imparts is a radiant revelation that flickers like a guiding star on our healing journey: "You cannot change your past, but you can change your future by changing your attitude towards your past."

These words, seemingly simple yet brimming with profound truth, are an invitation to embark on a transformative expedition within. The invitation calls us to release the grip of regret and resentment that the past might hold over us, freeing us from the relentless cycle of blame that binds us to the sorrows and hardships we've endured. The beauty lies not in denying the past's existence or erasing its scars, but in altering our perception of it – from a source of pain to a wellspring of lessons and growth. In these words, Apostle Selman alludes to the power of self-acceptance as a cornerstone of personal evolution. It's a recognition that we are not defined by the wounds of our history; rather, we are shaped by our response to them. The journey toward self-acceptance is a pilgrimage through our vulnerabilities, a pilgrimage that compels us to embrace our imperfections with the tenderness we would extend to a wounded friend. By cradling our flaws and challenges with empathy, we forge a harmonious connection with our past, allowing it to be a mosaic of experiences that have sculpted our present selves.

229

Central to this transformative journey is the alchemical art of forgiveness. Apostle Selman's words remind us that forgiveness is not a mere act of absolution for others, but a profound act of liberation for ourselves. Through forgiveness, we untether our souls from the heavy anchors of blame, liberating ourselves from the painful clutches of resentment that have held us captive. In this act, we pave the way for fresh beginnings, as the slate of our emotions is cleansed, allowing us to write our future with the ink of renewed purpose and unburdened hope. As we dissect these teachings, we encounter an invitation to step into the realm of empowerment. We are beckoned to confront the past not with bitterness, but with an unwavering determination to transmute it into a wellspring of strength. The attitude we adopt toward our past shapes our perspective, influencing how we navigate the present and shape our tomorrow. In embracing self-acceptance and forgiveness, we plant the seeds of transformation, nurturing a garden of resilience that blooms with every step we take forward.

Apostle Joshua Selman's wisdom encapsulates the essence of our human journey - a journey rife with trials and triumphs, sorrows and joys. Through his teachings, we grasp the compass that steers us toward a brighter horizon, where our past no longer holds us captive, but rather propels us toward a destiny shaped by the choices we make today. The shackles of blame are shattered, and we stride forward, fueled by the fire of acceptance and guided by the light of forgiveness, embracing the potential for growth and renewal that lies before us. Psychiatrist and author Gabor Mate shares valuable insights into the impact of early-life trauma on our emotional well-being. He reminds us, "Trauma is not what happens to us, but what we hold inside in the absence of an empathetic witness." Mate's words highlight the significance of seeking support and understanding from empathetic individuals during our healing process. The insightful words of psychologist and author Jordan Peterson resonate like a symphony of enlightenment, adding a profound layer to the ongoing narrative. His assertion, "If you don't say what you think, then you kill your unborn self," reaches into the depths of the human psyche, illuminating a path of self-discovery and transformation that is both poignant and invigorating. Within the context of navigating the treacherous terrains of trauma and blame, Peterson's wisdom becomes a compass guiding us to confront our past, voice our experiences, and unearth the seeds of personal growth.

Imagine our unexpressed thoughts and emotions as delicate, unformed embryos, waiting to be nurtured into existence. Peterson's words paint a vivid picture of the consequences of silence - the untold stories, the stifled emotions, and the stifled pain that, if left dormant, stagnate the very essence of who we are meant to become. This concept becomes particularly relevant when dealing with the weight of trauma and blame. Suppressing these feelings is akin to smothering the potential for healing and metamorphosis that lies within us. In the context of trauma, the words act as an invitation to shed the shadows of secrecy and silence that often accompany painful experiences. The act of speaking, or articulating our thoughts and emotions, is akin to bringing the ghosts of the past into the light. By doing so, we not only validate our own experiences but also cultivate a space for understanding and empathy from ourselves and others. Through vocalization, we permit ourselves to heal, to release the shackles of blame that might have held us captive for far too long. Furthermore, the wisdom encapsulated in Peterson's quote serves as a powerful reminder of the profound impact of confronting our past on the journey of personal growth. It underscores the transformative nature of speaking our truth, akin to tilling the fertile soil of our inner landscape. Through this courageous act, we allow dormant seeds of resilience and strength to awaken and flourish within us.

When we acknowledge and share our lived experiences, we set in motion a process of self-reclamation. We take the pen and begin rewriting the narrative that once ensnared us in endless cycles of blame and victimhood. This active engagement with our past is the catalyst for our evolution into a version of ourselves that is empowered and enriched by the wisdom born from acknowledging and embracing our unique journey. The simple act of giving voice to our thoughts and emotions becomes an embodiment of self-compassion and self-care. It's a powerful testament to our commitment to our own well-being, a declaration to ourselves that we deserve to be heard and understood. By breaking the suffocating silence that once bound us, we grant ourselves the permission to seek the support we need, whether it be through trusted friends, therapists, or support groups. This act not only strengthens our resolve to heal but also serves as a shining testament to our remarkable resilience and our boundless capacity for growth. In a world where the scars of trauma and the weight of blame can cast enduring shadows over our lives, it is imperative to acknowledge that the path to healing is both intricate and deeply personal. Recognizing this, we must understand that seeking professional help, engaging in therapy, or participating in support groups can be indispensable tools in surmounting these formidable challenges. Through these invaluable resources, we discover a haven of solace and understanding as we navigate the intricate and often arduous journey toward healing.

It is essential to remember that the pursuit of self-acceptance, forgiveness, and resilience demands unwavering patience and unrelenting perseverance. As we gradually come to embrace our past as an inseparable part of our unique journey, we unlock the doors to a future illuminated with possibility and hope. Let us not forget that the trials and tribulations life present need not define us. Instead, they can serve as the steppingstones that lead us toward a version of ourselves that is stronger, wiser, and profoundly empowered. Together, hand in hand, we have the capacity to rise above the traumas of the past and construct a future characterized by hope, compassion, and extraordinary growth. During my healing process of overcoming blame, I engaged in these four exercises. I encourage you to try them today, and with focus and intentionality, I am certain change will commence.

Self-Reflection And Journaling: Self-Reflection and Journaling have become my trusted companions on this winding journey of self-discovery and healing. They are the tools that have guided me through the labyrinthine corridors of my own mind, allowing me to delve deep into the recesses of my soul. In the quiet moments when pen meets paper, I find solace and clarity. I lay bare my thoughts and emotions, allowing them to unfurl like fragile petals of a long-dormant flower. It's in these words that I unearth the root causes of my blame, tracing the intricate threads of my past experiences that have woven themselves into the fabric of my being. Each stroke of the pen is an act of courage, a step toward self-compassion and acceptance. It's a process of untangling the knots that have bound me to my own suffering, a process of releasing the grip of blame that has held me captive for far too long.

In the sacred pages of my journal, I bear witness to the intricate dance of my thoughts and emotions, a journey of profound transformation. What once dwelled within me as resentment and blame has gracefully evolved into understanding and forgiveness. With each stroke of my pen, my journal becomes a testament to my resilience, an ode to my unwavering commitment to personal growth and well-being. In those tender moments of journaling, I do not merely recount my past; I rewrite the very narrative of my existence. I weave a tale liberated from the burdens of pain, infused instead with the luminous threads of hope and possibility. With each entry, I draw closer to the essence of self-discovery and the profound healing that awaits. In the embrace of my journal, I find solace and freedom. It is a sanctuary where I can explore the depths of my soul without judgment or restraint. With gratitude in my heart, I cherish the transformative power of journaling, knowing that within these pages lies the key to unlocking my innermost truths.

Practice Mindfulness and Meditation: Mindfulness and meditation have become the anchors of my daily life, guiding me towards a profound shift in perspective and a newfound sense of inner peace. In these practices, I have discovered the power of the present moment. Mindfulness teaches me to be fully present and to embrace the here and now with an open heart and a non-judgmental mind. It is a conscious act of observing my thoughts and emotions as they arise, without allowing them to define me or hold me captive. With each mindful breath, I release the tight grip of past grievances and create space for healing and transformation. Meditation, on the other hand, is my sanctuary of inner calm. It is the sacred space where I delve deep into the recesses of my soul, shedding light on the shadows that have fueled my blame and resentment. Through meditation, I cultivate a profound awareness of my inner landscape, gently unraveling the knots of negative emotions and replacing them with seeds of positivity and self-acceptance.

In these practices, I have discovered that the past no longer needs to dictate my present. I have learned to embrace each moment as an opportunity for growth and self-discovery. Mindfulness and meditation have allowed me to release the burdens of blame and resentment, nurturing a mindset that is more positive, forgiving, and accepting. As I sit in stillness, I am reminded that the power to change lies within me. It is through these practices that I have found the strength to let go of the past and embrace a future filled with hope and possibility.

Seek Professional Support: Therapists and counselors provide a sanctuary of understanding and support, a safe space where past traumas can be unraveled and examined with care. They are the skilled guides who equip us with coping strategies, offering a lifeline when we feel adrift in the tumultuous sea of our emotions. Through their expertise, we can cultivate a healthier perspective on life, one that is free from the burdens of the past. Not every mental health professional is the perfect fit, and it's crucial to find someone who understands our unique needs on multiple levels – cultural, metaphysical, geographical, and emotional. The therapeutic relationship is built on trust and connection, and it's only when we feel comfortable sharing our deepest vulnerabilities that true healing can occur. It is crucial to seek out a therapist or counselor who not only comprehends your struggles but also connects with you on a profound level. It's a step toward self-care and personal growth that can make all the difference on the path to healing and emotional well-being.

Engage In Creative Expression: Art, music, dance, or any form of creative expression can serve as a therapeutic outlet for emotions and pent-up feelings. Creative expression is indeed a powerful channel for processing emotions and fostering personal growth. Whether it's through art, music, dance, or any other form of creative outlet, these activities offer a sanctuary for our pent-up feelings and unspoken emotions.

I recalled engaging in an act of speaking to myself through different stages, recording thoughts, writing them in a journal, and then reciting them in the recording as a way to release what's been weighing on my heart and mind and serves as a means of self-reflection and self-understanding. It's a practice that allows me to externalize my inner turmoil and explore it in a safe and non-judgmental space. Art, music, dance, or any creative endeavor can serve as a sanctuary of self-expression, free from judgment. These activities invite us to explore our inner landscapes, to paint our emotions on a canvas, to dance to the rhythm of our hearts, or to compose melodies that resonate with our souls. In doing so, we create a safe space to confront and process our experiences, promoting healing and personal growth. The process of externalizing our emotions, whether through spoken word, written word, or other artistic forms, can be profoundly healing. It allows us to make sense of our experiences, to give voice to our feelings, and to witness our growth and evolution overcoming the pains of our past.

Cultivate Empowering Relationships: Surrounding yourself with supportive and understanding individuals is crucial in the journey to stop blaming and start living. Healthy relationships provide a sense of belonging, empathy, and encouragement, helping you break free from the cycle of blame and embrace a more positive outlook on life. Personally, I am grateful to my church pastor and family for their genuine support and understanding and I join groups such as United Kings and a few other groups who give me the platform to be vulnerable and express myself.

As you embark on this transformative journey, always remember the profound influence your thoughts hold in shaping your reality. By nurturing a mindset of self-compassion and growth, you cultivate fertile ground for profound transformation.

In closing, it's crucial to recognize that the path to release from blame is not one walked alone. It's a collective expedition, undertaken by individuals who dare to challenge the status quo and reclaim their agency. With the utmost sincerity, I extend this invitation to you, having personally witnessed the remarkable power of these exercises in my own life. As you take these steps today, know that the ripples of change you set in motion will gradually reshape your perspective, fortify your resilience, and illuminate the path toward a future marked by healing, growth, and empowerment. These activities, when incorporated into your life, can lead to a gradual transformation, allowing you to relinquish blame, embrace self-compassion, and embark on a profoundly fulfilling journey toward a brighter future.

In this transformative period, I decree and declare that your approach will be rewarded in every aspect of your being—mentally, physically, and emotionally. May you find the strength, healing, and growth you seek as you embark on this journey of self-discovery and personal empowerment. The future is yours to shape, and I have every confidence that you will do so with courage, resilience, and unwavering determination.

CONCLUSION

The Three Pillars of Unchaining the Past

L ife's countless experiences propel us into uncharted territories, shaping the course of our journey. These encounters, at times, mold our character, while at other times, they serve as trials that test our resilience. Nonetheless, as we endeavor to expand the networks of our comprehension amid the crucible of life's problems, we often find ourselves entangled in the shadows of mere survival, all while yearning for the fullness of true existence. Unbeknownst to us, this paradox imprisons us within the confines of our former selves, individuals shackled by a hidden secret or a haunting experience we dare not divulge. Our apprehension, shame, or the sheer incapacity to embrace the individuals that divinity intended us to be tethered to the specters of past heartbreaks, setbacks, failures, divorces, abuses, abandonments, or the harrowing memories of past wars. Yet, a profound truth emerges amidst this intricate process of constructing and deconstructing the essence of our existence. This truth, often grasped by only a select few and eluding the understanding of many, centers on fundamental questions that eventually occupy the thoughts of everyone: Who am I, and does the path I tread today align with a promising tomorrow?

The truth resides at the heart of both illumination and obscurity. It serves as the fulcrum upon which our understanding of reality hinges. Like a beacon of light, the truth has the power to dispel the darkness of ignorance and deception. It unveils the hidden, banishing the shadows of doubt and falsehood. Yet, paradoxically, the truth can be shrouded in darkness. It may conceal painful realities, uncomfortable truths, or our inner struggles. We often find ourselves reluctant to confront these hidden aspects of truth, fearing the emotional or psychological turmoil they may bring. In this intricate interplay between light and darkness, the truth emerges as a guiding force, inviting us to navigate the complexities of life. It challenges us to embrace both the brilliance of enlightenment and the shadows of introspection, recognizing that only by confronting all facets of truth can we hope to attain a deeper understanding of ourselves and the world around us. The narrative we present to the world, the image we craft, and the values we outwardly profess, while necessary, take a back seat to the internal dialogue we maintain with ourselves. When we genuinely convey our authentic selves to others, the words we speak, the eloquence of our delivery, or the veneer of sophistication become secondary. In authentic human interactions, especially among men who traditionally communicate through unspoken codes, the raw honesty resonates.

The power of such candid expression lies in its ability to reveal the words and the emotions, experiences, and vulnerabilities underlying them. In these moments, the truth takes precedence over artifice, and the connection between individuals transcends the superficial. Without the distractions of pretense or guile, we can recognize one another for who we are. In these unguarded exchanges, genuine human connections are forged, where the essence of our shared humanity is laid bare, and proper understanding and empathy can thrive. Truth is the key that unlocks the doors to liberation and self-discovery. It offers us a path to clarity in understanding ourselves and forms the foundation of our social connections, enriching our existence. Truth is not merely a concept; it is a force that extends our lifespans, connecting us to the universe and the universal principles of interconnectedness.

When we embrace truth, we unlock a multitude of rewards. It multiplies the potential of our actions, transforming the impact of one into the influence of millions. Truth aligns us with destiny's allies—those who help, finance, provide for, and complement our life journey. To lead an authentic life is to confront ourselves daily, our greatest rivals, with unwavering courage. It is to unapologetically confront uncomfortable truths, for only by being truthful to ourselves can we truly experience a life worth living, one marked by authenticity, vitality, and the boldness to face our inner challenges.

Our prayers can be seen as the medium through which we open channels for divine guidance and communication, just as truth is the gateway for confronting the shadows that tether us to our past. For many, the crucible of the COVID-19 pandemic became the catalyst that compelled them to confront uncomfortable truths about themselves and their circumstances. It was an internal struggle, a war of self-discovery. However, as we face our inner truths and emerge victorious in the battles that wage within us, the next crucial step is to cultivate faith. In Hebrews 11:1, the Bible beautifully defines faith as "the assurance of things hoped for, the conviction of things not seen." Faith is the catalyst that propels us beyond the scars of our past hurts.

Faith is the vital element that stirs up the courage to hope, believe, and envision the unseen possibilities that lie ahead, even before we reach our destination. It's akin to seeing the finish line from the start of the race. With faith, we navigate life's twists and turns, knowing that our convictions and hopes will guide us despite the uncertainty of what lies beyond the horizon. Truth and faith are intertwined; knowing the truth without faith renders our existence akin to a lifeless, hollow existence. Through faith, we breathe life into our realities, empowering us to overcome challenges, face adversity, and emerge as more robust, more resilient individuals.

Faith has been my guiding light through life's most profound and shadowed abysses. It is the beacon that has led me from a life expectancy shrouded in uncertainty, where merely reaching the age of 35 seemed like an improbable feat, to a life expectancy that stretches towards the horizon of 80 years. Faith has been my savior, my refuge, and my constant companion, rescuing me from the clutches of abuse, the frigid isolation of abandonment, the stark desolation of homelessness, the despairing neglect, the echoing chambers of loneliness, and the excruciating agony of pain. In the darkest hours of my existence, faith stood as an unwavering pillar, bolstering my courage and conviction that a brighter tomorrow awaited. Faith encouraged me to step into places I believed were beyond my reach, defying the shackles of doubt and insecurity that threatened to hold me back. In my battle against the abyss of depression, faith emerged as my armor, shielding me from the relentless onslaught of mental illness that sought to claim my very life.

The power of faith is an extraordinary force, one that cannot be underestimated. It extends beyond mere belief; it encompasses a profound awareness of self-empowerment, self-control, self-reliance, and self-discipline. Faith becomes the conduit through which we tap into the inherent power vested within us by the divine. Our boundless abilities to overcome adversity, heal emotional and psychological wounds, shatter the chains that bind us to the past, and transcend the limitations that once held us captive. Faith is the engine of resilience, propelling us forward when the world seems bleak and unforgiving. It fuels our determination to break through the barriers that obstruct our path and empowers us to overcome even the most formidable challenges life may hurl in our direction. With faith as our steadfast companion, we are not merely survivors but conquerors of our circumstances, sculptors of our destinies, and architects of our futures.

In the tapestry of human existence, faith weaves a thread of hope, connecting the present to the promises of a brighter, more fulfilling tomorrow. The radiant sunrise pierces the darkest night, the whisper of possibility that urges us to persist when all seems lost. Faith is the force that dares us to dream, aspire, and achieve beyond the boundaries of our perceived limitations. In essence, faith empowers us to write our own stories, to transform our weaknesses into strengths, and to emerge from the crucible of life not as victims of circumstance but as champions of our destinies. It is the steadfast belief that, with faith in ourselves and the indomitable power it bestows, there are no challenges too significant, no trials too arduous, and no darkness too profound to extinguish the light of hope burning within us.

We are extraordinary beings, each intricately crafted in the divine likeness. Our existence is not a haphazard occurrence, but a purposeful journey designed to unveil the depths of our potential and manifest every latent talent and aspiration within us. We are the living embodiment of a purposeful existence, destined to connect the dots on a cosmic canvas that stretches beyond the limits of perception. Our truth is the sacred portal to our innermost essence, the doorway to the wellspring of our inherent power. Through this truth, we unearth the reservoir of strength, creativity, and wisdom that lies dormant within our souls, waiting to be unleashed upon the world. When we embrace our truth, we embark on a profound journey of self-discovery that unveils the power within. Within each of us lies a reservoir of untapped potential, a wellspring of boundless power that transcends the ordinary and propels us into the realms of champions and legends. This power, the essence of our very being, is the epistle where our names are etched in the annals of greatness. It is within this inner sanctum that we find the strength to overcome the trials and tribulations of life, where pain, hurt, and suffering are transformed into the ink that writes our stories on the unending dotted line of existence.

Our journey toward healing and self-liberation is often marked by scars, leading us from despair to the heights of self-realization. It is a path of profound transformation, where we learn to love, lead, parent, and make decisions that reflect the wisdom gained from our trials. At the heart of this transformative journey lies the power of self, which allows us to recognize that our experiences, even the most traumatic, can be wielded as weapons of good rather than instruments of evil. Our inner power awakens us to the profound truth that the trials and suffering we endure are not meant to imprison us but to propel us forward. It teaches us that our true strength does not reside solely in the knowledge we acquire or the circumstances of our birth. Instead, our power is forged in the crucible of adversity, the fiery furnace of the challenges we overcome, and our unwavering determination to rise above the wounds inflicted upon us.

No matter how acute, today's pains are not destined to be everlasting. What endures is our agility, consistency, tenacity, and veracity—the qualities that drive us to persevere despite the mental, physical, emotional, verbal, sexual, or psychological abuse we may have endured. The realization that we are not defined by what happened to us but by what we have overcome empowers us to embrace our pain, confront our hurts, and defy the suffering that life may hurl our way. Amid our pain and suffering, we must acknowledge that we live in a world that can often be callous and unforgiving. Regardless of our race, wealth, geography, or religion, trauma is a shared human experience. If it has not touched us already, it may do so in the future. Our journeys toward healing may take different paths. Still, the three pillars that have fortified me in unchaining myself from the shackles of the past to embrace parenthood, leadership, love, and decisive decision-making are Truth, Faith, and Power.

Truth is the bedrock upon which our healing journey is built. It enables us to discern what is reality and what is a distorted perception. By confronting our truths, we unveil the authentic narrative of our lives, dispelling the myths that may have shrouded our understanding of ourselves and our experiences. Faith, the second pillar, opens the door to a horizon of possibility. It allows us to recognize that we can overcome adversity, heal, and grow. Faith is the beacon that guides us through the darkest nights of the soul, reminding us that even in our most vulnerable moments, there is hope and resilience within us.

The third pillar, the Power within, is the furnace where our strength is forged. It burns away the layers of complexity and uncertainty, simplifying the intricacies of our existence into the dotted lines of life. This inner power dismantles the chains that bind us to our past, liberating us to become the architects of our future. In the crucible of these three pillars—Truth, Faith, and Power, we find the arsenals to combat the scars of our past and the challenges that the future may hold. Our trials and tribulations are no longer seen as obstacles to our happiness but as steppingstones to greater heights. With these pillars as our foundation, we move forward with the unwavering belief that our past does not define our destiny but by the boundless potential of our inner power. We are not victims of circumstance; we are champions and legends in the making, etching our stories onto the unending dotted line of life.

I must admit that sharing life experiences has been both gut-wrenching and relieving. However, it underscores the power of confronting our truths, having faith in our potential, and tapping into the inner strength that resides within us. Our life experiences and the wisdom we've gained serve as a wellspring of inspiration for those navigating their challenges and seeking a path to healing and self-realization. Sharing our stories is a profound means of connecting with others, offering hope, and breaking free from the mental loops of trauma that can hold us back. When we open up about our experiences, it's not only a source of inspiration for those who hear our stories, but it also fosters the creation of a supportive and empathetic community where healing can flourish.

While my journey is uniquely mine, and yours may be similar or different, it's essential to recognize that every person's journey is distinct. By sharing our experiences, we aid in our personal healing and contribute to a collective narrative of resilience and transformation. This collective narrative can help create a more compassionate and understanding world for future generations, enabling them to prosper and thrive.

As we conclude this excerpt, we recognize it as not just an ending, but the dawn of a new beginning. May my journey serve as a beacon of inspiration, urging you to embrace boldness, break free from constraints, and live authentically. I am emboldened by the realization of life's impermanence, prompting us to clear the canvas of our existence and trust in our inherent significance. Let us internalize the power of freedom, both within and without, and hold steadfast to the belief in our own greatness. With persistence, we shall ascend to even greater heights, fueled by the truth, faith, and divine power bestowed upon us.

Thank you for embarking on this journey with me, may the light of compassion and understanding guide your deeds, and may your words continue to ignite inspiration in those around you. May your path be paved with continuous growth and fulfillment.

ABOUT THE AUTHOR

The author, Joshua Kennedy epitomizes a remarkable fusion of compassion, dedication, and resilience, setting him apart as an exceptional individual across multiple spheres of life. Rooted deeply in his faith as a devout Christian, Joshua's values serve as guiding principles, shaping his roles as a nurturing father to four remarkable boys, a devoted partner, and a cherished son and brother. In his professional capacities as both a Social Worker and Clinical Therapist, Joshua exhibits unwavering commitment to enhancing the lives of others. His blend of compassion and expertise equips him to offer invaluable support to individuals grappling with challenges, empowering them to embark on journeys towards healing and holistic well-being.

Beyond his professional endeavors, Joshua's philanthropic spirit radiates through his dedicated volunteering efforts, particularly in underprivileged and underserved communities, with a focus on Liberia. His fervent belief in the transformative power of education fuels his passion for fostering educational advancement, as he tirelessly endeavors to uplift and empower disadvantaged children. Propelled by a profound sense of purpose and gratitude for his calling, Joshua views life's adversities as opportunities for growth and resilience. His contagious optimism and unwavering enthusiasm for personal development inspire those around him, both in face-to-face interactions and through his active presence on social media platforms.

Joshua's genuine desire to uplift and motivate others, coupled with his extensive experience and steadfast commitment to service, solidify his reputation as a catalyst for positive change. His ability to thrive amidst challenges and his innate capacity to forge meaningful connections make him a beacon of hope and inspiration in his community and beyond. For further engagement and inspiration, individuals are encouraged to connect with Joshua on social media platforms under the handle @KennedyMotivate, where his uplifting messages continue to resonate and inspire countless others on their own journeys of personal and professional growth.

Made in the USA
Middletown, DE
19 March 2024

51313999R00146